D1187319

WITHDRAWN

PIERS PLOWMAN

AN INTRODUCTION

By ELIZABETH SALTER

Professor of Mediaeval English Literature
University of York

CALVIN T. RYAN LIBRARY
U. OF NEBRASKA AT KEARNEY

BASIL BLACKWELL
OXFORD
1969

© *Basil Blackwell & Mott, Ltd., 1962*

First edition 1962
Reprinted 1963
Second edition 1969

Cloth edition
631   12370   9

Paperback edition
631   12380   6

Library of Congress Catalogue
Card Number: 71–95554

Printed by offset in Great Britain
by Alden & Mowbray Ltd
at the Alden Press, Oxford
and bound at Kemp Hall Bindery

PREFACE

MY grateful acknowledgements are due to Professor Phyllis Hodgson, who first helped me towards an understanding of *Piers Plowman*: to Dr. J. A. W. Bennett, whose advice and criticism in the formative stages of this book have been invaluable: to Professor Bruce Dickins, whose friendly vigilance has so often saved me from error: to Sir Basil Blackwell, whose patience and courtesy have been unfailing: and to the many Cambridge students with whom I have discussed Langland in recent years.

The jacket illustration is taken, by kind permission of the British Museum, from a reproduction of the Luttrell Psalter, made in 1340 for Sir Geoffrey Luttrell of Irnham, Lincolnshire.

E.S.

1962

CONTENTS

PIERS PLOWMAN

CHAPTER I

THE APPROACH

THE most important reason for reading *Piers Plowman* is its magnificence as a work of religious art; conceived greatly, it contains a wider variety of fine poetry than any other work from the English Middle Ages. Langland's inquiry into man's relationship with God, set in the powerful allegory of the search which ends only to begin afresh, is not challenged for span and strength of execution by anything in English literature except *Paradise Lost*. Both poems have the same broad spiritual landscape. Milton's 'dungeon horrible' and 'opal towrs and battlements' are those which Langland saw as he passed from waking life on the Malvern Hills to his dream of 'a toure on a toft. trielich ymaked; a depe dale binethe. a dongeon there-inne', and their vision moves constantly between Heaven and Hell, with Earth as the battleground of divine and devilish agencies. Both, moreover, are shaped as the prelude to a further drama—a drama to be worked out within each responsible human being. In the closing lines of *Piers Plowman* and *Paradise Lost* we are certainly conscious of the immense backward stretch of all that has been suffered and achieved, and yet we know that this is only the beginning; great vistas of thought and action still open before us. As the poems end, new pilgrimages are about to take place; *Piers Plowman* shows us Conscience resolving upon a journey:

'Bi Cryste,' quod Conscience tho. 'I will bicome a pilgryme,
And walken as wyde. as al the worlde lasteth,
To seke Piers the Plowman. that Pryde may destruye,
. . . . now Kynde me auenge,
And sende me happe and hele. til I haue Piers the Plowman.'[1]

[1] *The Vision of William concerning Piers the Plowman, in Three Parallel Texts*, ed. W. W. Skeat (Oxford, 1881), 2 vols., reprinted in 1954 with a Bibliographical note by Dr. J. A. W. Bennett. Quotation is made from this edition throughout unless otherwise noted. Of the three existing versions of the poem, the so-called A, B, and C texts, the B text has been taken as the basis for literary discussion; dated about 1377, and containing a Prologue and twenty Passus, it provides the most complete version of the poem, and is the text usually encountered on a first reading. See the Appendix for a brief outline of the nature and relationship of the three texts and the Bibliography for a list of editions.

Any critical study has to bear in mind that textual work upon the poem is still in progress. Of the definitive editions now in preparation, only that of the early A text has been published: *Will's Visions of Piers Plowman and Do-wel*, ed. G. Kane (London, 1960). It seems unlikely, however, that the poem will emerge so altered as to invalidate general literary comment based upon Skeat's edition.

In *Paradise Lost* two pilgrims set out:

> They looking back, all th' Eastern side beheld
> Of Paradise, so late their happie seat,
> Waved over by that flaming brand, the gate
> With dreadful Faces throng'd, and fierie Arms:
> Some natural Tears they drop'd, but wip'd them soon:
> The world was all before them, where to choose
> Their place of rest, and Providence their guide:
> They hand in hand with wandering steps and slow
> Through Eden took their solitarie way.

But if the basic purpose of both poets might be expressed in Milton's words—the need to 'assert Eternal Providence, And justifie the wayes of God to men'—their art offers no such grounds for comparison. It is Langland's peculiar distinction that, at one and the same time, he can keep us fully in touch with the great metaphysical consequences of human existence and with the tangible realities of our humorous, corrupt, frustrating and yet desirable life on earth. The language in which he conveys deep spiritual truths:

> 'For I, that am lorde of lyf.loue is my drynke,
> And for that drynke to-day.I deyde vpon erthe.'
> (B.XVIII.363-4)

is often as simple and familiar as that in which he invites his reader to share the experience of the mediaeval peasant's harsh life in wintertime, the warm, raucous atmosphere of the alehouse:

> Kokes and here knaues.crieden, 'hote pyes, hote!
> Good goos and grys.go we dyne, gowe!'
> Tauerners 'a tast for nouht'.tolden the same,
> 'Whit wyn of Oseye.and of Gascoyne,
> Of the Ruele and of the Rochel wyn.the roste to defye.'[1]
> (C.I.226-230)

Praising Christ who 'blewe alle thi blissed   into the blisse of paradise', he achieves that blend of reverence and vigour which few religious writers after the mediaeval period were capable of, and which was not put to such high poetic uses by any of Langland's contemporaries. Sharp forthrightness of diction and spontaneity of verse-movement give us often a direct entry into *Piers Plowman*: much of the verse provides reading quite as unhampered as any we are likely to meet in the work of Chaucer, for instance, or in the Miracle Plays. And because of the return of many twentieth-century poets to the use of the free, unrhymed, accentual line which

---

[1] '. . . to help your meat settle.'

is Langland's verse norm, we can often respond to the movement of *Piers Plowman* as to a contemporary verse pattern. Familiarity with the characteristic rhythms of Pound, Eliot, Auden, means that lines such as these

> 'And that falleth to the fader.that formed vs alle,
> Loked on vs with loue.and lete his sone deye
> Mekely for owre mysdedes.to amende vs all;'
>
> (B.I.164–6)

need no special introduction as 'mediaeval verse': they come naturally and simply to the listener. Moreover the conviction that no theme and no vocabulary are to be debarred from poetry on account of their closeness to everyday, ordinary life, is one from which spring some of the finest passages in *Piers Plowman* as well as some of the finest in compositions nearer to our own day. 'For the modern poet nothing is inherently unpoetic';[1] this observation could be made equally well about Langland, as he presses sights, experiences and words, with little or no special selection, into the service of his urgent and dedicated purpose.

But it is not possible to recommend Langland as a poet who is always accessible to present-day readers. There *are* times when his work raises problems for us—problems only capable of partial solution by reference to contemporary thought and artistic methods. For *Piers Plowman* is 'English mediaeval' in ways that Chaucer's poetry, drawing strongly on French and Italian cultural traditions, could never be. If, therefore, we are to gain more than a partial understanding of Langland's art and meaning, we have to be prepared to meet a challenge almost as often as a welcome. It is easy to select and praise 'star' poetic passages, such as the splendid speech of Christ after the Harrowing of Hell:

> 'For I, that am lorde of lyf.loue is my drynke,
> And for that drynke to-day.I deyde vpon erthe.
> I faughte so, me threstes ʒet.for mannes soule sake;
> May no drynke me moiste.ne my thruste slake,
> Tyl the vendage falle.in the vale of Iosephath,
> That I drynke righte ripe must.*resureccio mortuorum*,[2]
> And thanne shal I come as a kynge.crouned with angeles,
> And han out of helle.alle mennes soules.'
>
> (B.XVIII.363–370)

---

[1] C. Day Lewis, *The Poetic Image* (London, 1951), p. 106.
[2] 'No drink shall moisten me, nor slake my thirst until the time of vintage in the vale of Jehoshaphat when I shall drink of the ripe new wine, the resurrection of the dead.'

There are many of equal dignity and beauty. It is also easy to find reasons for praising the whole work which are not sufficiently profound or comprehensive. *Piers Plowman* has been, and still is, read as a satirical commentary on the mediaeval scene, as a subtly performed exercise in religious allegory, or as a deepening analysis and correction of sin. It is much more difficult to grasp the poem as a total religious and artistic unit, operating extensively and harmoniously according to laws which may not be entirely familiar to us either from modern literature, or from the better known departments of mediaeval literature. The difficulty, however, should not deter us, for the rewards are unusually rich. *Piers Plowman* is a poem unique in its period. Connected with and resembling many other mediaeval literary forms, it is *exactly* like none of them; drawing fully upon the great common stock of mediaeval religious doctrines and images, it reinterprets and renews what it takes in the light of a highly personal vision.

The fact that so many different ways of approaching Langland's work can be recommended should be accepted as a sign of its wealth of content, and not as a persuasion to assert the exclusive truth of any one particular way. Each is justifiable, but not in isolation. The social-historical approach, for instance, which is the oldest-established, and uses the poem as a lively witness to the eventful years of the later fourteenth century, has a limited truth to convey.[1] From the satirical, dramatic parts of the poem, comes information on life and manners in mediaeval days; scenes from ale-houses, from the courts of Kings and Bishops, from country cottages, churches and London streets crowd one against the other. On the many pilgrimages we make throughout the poem, we notice the faces and conditions of men of Langland's time—the wealth and corruption, Church and State laid ruthlessly open to our view. Here we can learn of the bare, staple diet of a mediaeval country-man:

> '. . . two grene cheses,
> A few cruddes and creem. and an hauer cake,[2]
> And two loues of benes and bran...'
>
> (B.VI.283–5)

[1] See for instance, D. Chadwick, *Social Life in the Days of Piers Plowman* (C.U.P., 1922), and J. J. Jusserand, *English Wayfaring Life in the Middle Ages*, tr. L. T. Smith (London, 1889, reprinted 1950).
[2] '. . . and an oaten-cake.'

of the elaborate dress of a mediaeval noblewoman:

> Hire robe was ful riche. of red scarlet engreyned,
> With ribanes of red golde. and of riche stones . . .
>
> (B.II.15–16)

of the hunting parson, the deformed beggars, with their idle songs, 'How, trollilolli', and of the great, worldly Cardinals:

> 'The contre is the curseder. that cardynales come inne:'
>
> (B.XIX.415)

Piers Plowman tells us what an intelligent man of the late fourteenth-century thought of politics and institutions in his day; Langland was deeply moved by such issues as social injustice, the responsibilities of kingship, and comments directly upon them.

But when we have realized the contemporary scene through his words, we are in a position to make only a superficial judgement of Langland's work as a poet; we have hardly begun to grasp his meaning and appreciate his art. Langland's whole intention is not to offer a faithful record of his time, to be used as documentary evidence by later historians, and we must enlarge our view of the poem if our reading and comment is not to be limited and often irrelevant.

At the opposite end of the scale, we can approach the poem as an exercise in interpreting mediaeval religious allegory. This is, of course, an extremely important element in our total experience of *Piers Plowman*; it is necessary that we should proceed further than the literal story and attempt to penetrate to deeper meanings. The knights, beggars, prelates, and above all, the main figure of the poem, the plowman Piers himself, are part of a larger pattern of significance than that immediately discernible from their discussions and actions. Our minds must be conditioned to expect and to find at many points in the poem, 'multiple meaning'. And we have received great help here in recent years from critics whose endeavour it has been to show us the unfolding and resolution of Langland's allegory.[1]

There are signs, however, that we have perhaps turned too far away from the 'social-historical realism' to the complex symbolism

---

[1] Still most important among the many articles on the allegory are H. W. Wells, 'The Construction of Piers Plowman' and 'The Philosophy of Piers Plowman', *P.M.L.A.*, XLIV (9129) and LIII (1938), and N. Coghill, 'The Character of Piers the Plowman', *M. Aev.*, II (1933). E. T. Donaldson, in *Piers Plowman; The Poet of the C Text* (New Haven, 1949), Chapter VI, writes on the working of the allegory in the last version of the poem.

of the poem. In many ways we are only slightly nearer to understanding its nature, and Langland's intentions, if we account for
Piers Plowman as a consistently subtle exposition of spiritual truths,
made in the many-layered fashion best exemplified by mediaeval
Biblical commentary—literal, tropological, allegorical and anagogical senses packed tightly into the lines, only waiting to be
released by the watchful reader.[1] While there is no need to question
multiple meaning as an element in the work,[2] Langland's allegorical
usages are varied and fluctuating, and we cannot easily generalize
about the depth of significance in any given line of his verse.
Moreover, we must be sure that we are not supporting the claims
of the poetry by the interest of the allegory alone, and, in particular,
that we are not excusing faulty art by the same means. Whether
we are defending or attacking Langland's work, we must begin by
acknowledging that an absorbing allegory need not necessarily be a
great poem.

How, then, does the third commonly accepted way of reading
Piers Plowman—as an extensive versified sermon[3]—improve, if at all,
upon these methods? There is no denying its strong sermon
connections. The subject matter is often directly that of the
mediaeval pulpit; the didactic impulse in Langland is powerful.
Sermons are constantly being preached throughout the poem—
by the poet, by his characters. But we must be careful how we
express the relationship of *Piers Plowman* to sermon. A reduction
of the poem to the status of a better-than-usual mediaeval homily,
or series of homilies, is false and damaging; Langland utilizes
homiletic material and form to a considerable extent, but his
poem works through sermon to conclusions outside the reach of
sermon. An investigation of general likenesses to homiletic language
and procedure can, however, be of help in defining one particular
aspect of the poem—its art.

[1] The most extreme study of this kind is by D. W. Robertson and B. F. Huppé, *Piers
Plowman and Scriptural Tradition* (Princeton, 1951).
[2] As does Professor R. W. Frank in his study, *Piers Plowman and the Scheme of Salvation*
(New Haven, 1957), 'I shall read the poem as a literal rather than an allegorical poem and I
shall be looking for literal rather than hidden, second or higher meanings' (p. 2). This
approach is supported by Professor M. W. Bloomfield, in 'Symbolism in Mediaeval Literature',
M.P., LVI, No. 2 (1958).
[3] The comments by Professor G. R. Owst in *Literature and Pulpit in Mediaeval England*
(C.U.P., 1933) are extremely valuable; they do not, however, in my opinion penetrate
deeply enough into Langland's purpose. For a very recent 'sermon' view of the poem, see
the translation of *Piers Plowman* by Donald and Rachel Attwater (Everyman, 1957) '. . . it is
a good tract, a bit of moralist's work well done . . .' (Introduction, p. viii).

A reading of *Piers Plowman* which neglects the fact that this is essentially a work of art, a product of the creative imagination, is seriously restricted. And this holds good even if we are reading for the sake of content only, for the impulses of the poetry, the varying sound of the language, the graph of rhythm, are sensitive guides to minute and important fluctuations of meaning. It has taken much longer for critics to come to terms with Langland's poetry than with the substance of his work.[1] And it is not all the fault of critic and reader. Langland tells us frequently that he has vital matter to convey; only once does he speak of his 'poetic art'.[2] While his best poetry asks for no defence, there are times when we may feel, initially, more doubtful about Langland's claims to the title of 'poet'. Here our assumptions about what we are likely to find in a work such as *Piers Plowman* need some thought. A man of Langland's time, training and temperament would accept without question that art must serve devotion; the lowering of purely artistic standards on some occasions will be sanctioned and deliberate. But we should remember that the religious impulse can also be expected to generate poetic energy.[3] We must not be disposed, by criteria inappropriate to religious art, to find a tension in *Piers Plowman* between matter and form. Although we may ultimately be forced to accuse Langland of paying less attention to his art than to his meaning, of writing sense but failing to write poetry, we are not entitled to pass judgement unless we have prepared ourselves to receive a comprehensive work of a special poetic nature. We are not likely to feel deep and continuous pleasure in Langland's writing if we have not grasped the basic principle to which it works—the inseparability of religious and artistic forces—and, moreover, if we have not attempted to see it in its own context of space and time.

Approaching the poem, perhaps for the first time, we should take our directions from Langland himself. *Piers Plowman* is planned, as the opening lines tell us, on a cosmic scale: its dream province spans Earth, Heaven and Hell:

[1] The most helpful criticism of Langland's art comes from Professor G. Kane, *Middle English Literature* (London, 1951), Chapter III, from E. T. Donaldson, *op. cit.*, Chapter III, and from Professor J. Lawlor, *Piers Plowman. An Essay in Criticism* (London, 1962).

[2] See below, pp. 27 foll.

[3] See the important remarks by Susanne Langer in *Feeling and Form* (London, 1953), p. 402. 'In an age when art is said to serve religion, religion is really serving art. Whatever is holy to people inspires artistic conception.'

And merueylously me mette[1].as ich may ʒow telle;
Al the welthe of this worlde.and the woo bothe,
Wynkyng as it were.wyterly ich saw hyt,
Of tryuthe and of tricherye.of tresoun and of gyle,
Al ich saw slepynge.as ich shal ʒow telle.
Esteward ich byhulde.after the sonne,
And saw a toure, as ich trowede . truthe was ther-ynne;
Westwarde ich waitede[2].in a whyle after,
And sawe a deep dale.deth, as ich lyuede,
Wonede in tho wones[3].and wyckede spiritus.
A fair feld, ful of folke.fonde ich ther bytwyne,
Alle manere of men.the mene and the ryche,
Worchynge and wandrynge.as the worlde asketh.

(C.I.9–21)

And its theme is fittingly large; phrased many times over the course of the poem, it comes, in Passus I as a simple question, asked by the Dreamer:

'Teche me to no tresore.but telle me this ilke,
How I may saue my soule.that seynt art yholden?'

(B.I.83–4)

and answered by Holy Church:

'Loue is leche of lyf.and nexte owre lorde selue,
And also the graith gate.that goth into heuene;'[4]

(B.I.203–4)

Clearly Piers Plowman will be more than a social commentary or a religious satire; the spiritual journey to which the dreamer, and reader, are being introduced will be different from a Canterbury Pilgrimage—they seek, not a 'holy blisful martyr' but God himself. Though there will be many halts and detours, the road they must travel is 'the graith gate that goth into hevene': it will be arduous and exhilarating.

Then, too, we see early on that the poem is cast allegorically. Langland will often intend more than at first he appears to do; there will be a special associative power in some, though not all, of his plainest words. While we need not press too consistently for 'multiple meaning', we can assume that nothing in the world of the poem rests in simple isolation. We must not be halted for overlong by the picture of grotesque sin—here, of Avarice:

[1] 'And I dreamed wondrously . . .'   [2] 'I looked towards the west . . .' . .'
[3] '. . . lived in those dwellings . . .'
[4] 'Love is life's physician, and next to our Lord himself, and also the highway leading to heaven.'

He was bitelbrowed.and baberlipped also,
With two blered eyghen.as a blynde hagge;
And as a letheren purs.lolled his chekes,
Well sydder than his chyn.thei chiueled for elde;[1]
And as a bondman of his bacoun.his berde was bidraueled.
With a hode on his hed.a lousi hatte aboue,
And in a tauny tabarde.of twelue wynter age,
Al totorne and baudy.and ful of lys crepynge;

(B.V.190–197)

or the compassionate picture of beast and man, hungry and cold in winter time:

'And moche murthe in Maye is.amonges wilde bestes,
And so forth whil somer lasteth.her solace dureth.
Ac beggeres aboute Midsomer.bredlees thei soupe,
And ȝit is wynter for hem worse.for wete-shodde thei gange,
A-fyrst sore and afyngred.and foule yrebuked,
And arated of riche men.that reuthe is to here.[2]
Now, lorde, sende hem somer.and some maner Ioye,
Heuene after her hennes-goynge.that here han suche defaute!'

(B.XIV.158–165)

These are good examples of realistic art, but they have not, in this poem, a separate existence; they are part of a larger web of allegorical significances, which Langland can only help us to understand if we will accept the initial premise—a potentional though fluctuating richness of connected meanings.

And this is easier to accept if we remember that *Piers Plowman* is a dream poem. Within his 'merueilouse sweuene' Langland, the poet and thinker, is free to work as he wishes; if we, and his dreamer, seem to be subject to an unseen authority which moves us, sometimes inexplicably, from one scene or mode of meaning to another, this is surely nothing unusual for dream-experience. The events and thoughts in which we share will often, as in a *real* dream, have no more precise definition than that provided by the mere facts of sleeping and waking. Moreover, this is a dream whose religious nature becomes more significant as the poem continues; the abandonment of ordinary, rational logic is made more willingly when it is clear that deep spiritual revelation follows.

As for the nature, the quality of the poetry, we have only to attend closely as Langland introduces his themes, to realize that a man so oriented towards 'other heuene than here' will regard his

---

[1] '. . . they trembled with age, (sagging) well below his chin;'
[2] '. . . and abused by rich men in a pitiable manner', lit. 'that pity it is to hear of it'

B

art in a special way. He will demand that it achieve a blend of beauty and usefulness; its characteristic faults and excellences will depend intimately upon devotional needs. We must, therefore, understand how the mediaeval religious poet works—neither falling, on the one hand, into the error of supposing him to be hopelessly shackled by his faith, nor, on the other, ignoring the factors which may account for both his successes and limitations as an artist. More specifically, we can see how Langland drew upon certain long-established literary traditions to serve his vision. Born in a part of England where alliterative verse was a natural mode, he continued, even in the London of Chaucer's day, to write alliteratively. But he was equally indebted to the language and techniques of the mediaeval pulpit, and we can observe how both traditions combine, in an unusual, perhaps a unique way, to sanction his 'ars poetica'.

Piers Plowman has a large meaning which is accessible to us in its fullness provided that we are willing to use watchfulness and patience. It demands that we listen carefully to the poetry—the turn and flow of rhythm, the pattern of sound—and that we submit ourselves to the powerful working of the poet's imagination as phrase, image, and episode accumulate, enriching each other, and persuading us towards the acceptance of great general truths. For however absorbing it can become as an intellectual study, *Piers Plowman* claims out attention most strongly as a work of the religious imagination. Langland knows that

. . . the painted slide, the imagined ideal is the real: but it is only actual, only operative, when we see its image projected upon the transience and terror of our world.[1]

And his projection of the ideal onto the transient, terror-stricken world of the Field Full of Folk (which is our world too) calls out both art and devotion in a specially powerful way. So we see Gluttony, not simply as a vice or as a dramatic character, but as a principle of evil, able and waiting to take innumerable forms of life. In addition to many abstract sermons on the value of Patience and Humility, we witness the feast to which Patience and the Dreamer go: there the pathetic and amusing sight of these two lowly ones enduring, while the great Doctor of Divinity crams food and wine into himself, is turned by a single arrogant gesture into a revelation of sin:

[1] C. Day Lewis, *The Poetic Image*, p. 154.

'What is Dowel? sire doctour,' quod I, 'is Dowel any penaunce?'
'Dowel?' quod this doctour— and toke the cuppe and dranke—
(B.XIII.102–3)

Moreover, in the central sections of the poem, Langland adds to the preacher's exposition of God's love, a vision of Piers—Christ, taken and crucified, and risen from the dead, speaking to us, and involving us in the everlasting sacrifice of love. The poet who dreamed himself into a wilderness, 'wiste I neuer where', is found, in the end, 'speaking no dream, but things oracular'.

CHAPTER II

THE ART OF *PIERS PLOWMAN*:
ALLITERATIVE POEM, SERMON AND VISION

NO one has ever denied the interest of *Piers Plowman*, but only recently has it been defended wholeheartedly for its artistic merits. It was certainly popular in its own time and during the two centuries following;[1] there are over fifty manuscripts from the fourteenth and fifteenth centuries, and it was printed four times before 1561.[2] By the early sixteenth century, however, the enthusiasm for it had begun to concentrate on satiric material useful for the pillorying of social and religious abuses. And so it comes about, ironically, that a work so fundamentally Catholic and ortho-dox was used as a support for the Reformation:

> . . . it pleased God to open the eyes of many to se hys truth, geving them boldenes of herte, to open their mouthes and crye oute agaynste the worckes of darckenes, as did John Wicklefe . . . and this writer . . .[3]

The same editor urges his readers to persevere with the difficult language of the poem in order to come at the 'sence'. During our own century we have corrected the view which took into account only Langland's subject matter, but we are a long way from a satisfactory assessment of Langland as a poet.

There are sympathetic studies of *Piers Plowman* which are limited or biased in their interpretations of the poem because they do not consider sufficiently what Langland tells us by means of his poetry[4] and there are those which, however anxious to deal with art as well as sense, fail to understand fully the principles on which this particular kind of art is based.[5] The uncertainty of the position is reflected even in the thorough-going commendations of Langland

---

[1] See Professor Kane's remarks in the introduction to his edition of the A text: '*Piers Plowman* was a living text; its content was a matter of immediacy to a man reading, or reading and copying it during the fourteenth or fifteenth century' (p. 136).

[2] Printed in 1550, *The Vision of Pierce Plowman, now fyrste imprynted by Roberte Crowley, dwellyng in Ely rentes in Holburne*: *Anno Domini* 1505 (for 1550) and reprinted twice in that year. Reprinted again by Owen Rogers in 1561.

[3] Crowley, *op. cit.*, Preface.

[4] Miss G. Hort's *Piers Plowman and Contemporary Religious Thought* (London, 1938) and, more recently, the work of Robertson and Huppé and that of Frank (*op. cit.* above, p. 6) seem to me to suffer in this way.

[5] Some of the criticisms made in Professor Kane's chapter on 'Piers Plowman' in *Middle English Literature* seem to me questionable for this reason.

as a poet; claims are sometimes set too high. One recent lecture allows no room for any criticism of Langland's powers of expression[1] and too often excuses are made for what must be recognized as negligent (perhaps *deliberately* negligent) workmanship on the grounds of allegorical subtlety. But the responsibility for inferior writing in this poem cannot be shifted entirely from Langland to the uninstructed or unperceptive reader. Some stabilization of critical approach is clearly necessary.

(i) *The alliterative poem*

Any consideration of Langland's art must first deal with him as a poet of the 'alliterative tradition'. By adopting the unrhymed alliterative line as the basic metrical form for his work, Langland associated himself with those mediaeval poets of the west and north of England who inherited this method of composition from pre-Conquest times, and used it in preference to French-inspired metres.[2] Chaucer's comment on alliterative verse—given dramatically in the Prologue to the *Parson's Tale*—may or may not have a contemptuous note in it:

> But trusteth wel, I am a Southren man,
> I kan nat geeste 'rum, ram, ruf', by lettre[3]

But it shows that poets of London and the south, contemporary with Langland, did not find alliterative writing the most natural of modes; Chaucer rarely drops into alliteration, and, when he does, it is usually accommodated within his normal rhymed verse line.[4] Only scanty evidence is available about Langland's life and origins;[5] according to a memorandum on the last page of one manuscript of the poem, he was the son of 'Stacy de la Rokele,

[1] A. G. Mitchell, *Lady Meed and the Art of Piers Plowman* (University College, London, Chambers Memorial Lecture, 1956).
[2] The history of this 'alliterative continuity', seen in prose and verse, is to be found in R. W. Chambers, *On the Continuity of English Prose* (London, 1932), R. M. Wilson, *Early Middle English Literature* (London, 1939) and J. P. Oakden, *Alliterative Poetry in Middle English* (Part II) *A Survey of the Traditions* (Manchester, 1935).
[3] *Works*, ed. F. N. Robinson (O.U.P., 1957), p. 272.
[4] See D. Everett, 'Chaucer's "Good Ear"' in *Essays on Middle English Literature* (Oxford, 1955), pp. 139 foll.
[5] The controversies about single or multiple authorship of the three versions of the poem, the so-called A, B, and C texts, are not discussed in this study; sufficient scholarly evidence has been produced to support the near certainty, that one man, William Langland, was responsible for the whole. See G. Kane, *Piers Plowman. The Evidence for Authorship* (University of London, Athlone Press, 1965).

gentleman, of Shipton-under-Wychwood, Oxfordshire'.[1] Born about 1330, he spent his early years in the west country, around Ledbury and Malvern; while still a young man, in minor orders, he left for London, and there most of *Piers Plowman* must have been written. The London scene is often indicated in the poem— the law-courts of Westminster, Eastcheap, Tyburn, Southwark, the Thames—and in one waking interlude, we are told of the poet's house and family in the Cornhill district:

> Thus ich a-waked, god wot. whanne ich wonede on Cornehulle,
> Kytte and ich in a cote . . .
>
> (C.VI.1–2)

The poem begins, however, with Langland wandering 'on Maluerne hulles'. It opens out from a dream with a setting which is, no doubt, mainly literary—spring-morning, splashing stream, bank, sunlight, are all familiar introductory elements in mediaeval dream poetry[2]—but which may also have some more personal reference, back to the poet's youth in the west country. There, perhaps, his visions which were to remain with him until old age, began, and if the Malvern Hills are hardly mentioned again,[3] this may be because the poem represents, not in precise autobiographical detail, but more generally, a whole life of spiritual search and discovery. Writing in London, Langland continued to use the metre he could only have first learnt in the west, and the poem is shaped, to some extent, as a characteristic alliterative work.

What are we, then, to expect from a mediaeval poem which begins in so leisurely and sonorous a manner:

> In a somer seson. whan soft was the sonne,
> I shope me in shroudes. as I a shepe were . . .[4]
>
> (B.Prol.1–2)

---

[1] The MS. is Trinity College, Dublin, D.4.1. See E. St. John Brooks, 'The *Piers Plowman* Manuscripts in Trinity College, Dublin', *The Library*, 5th Series, vol. vi (1951). The best biographical treatment of Langland is to be found in E. Talbot Donaldson's *Piers Plowman* (*op. cit.*) Chapter VII. See also Kane, *Evidence for Authorship*, op. cit.

[2] The most famous of the French dream-poems, the thirteenth-century *Roman de la Rose*, has a dream landscape set in sunny May weather, with bird-song and rushing waters, which Chaucer adapts for his early poem, the *Book of the Duchess*. But Langland is anticipated more nearly by several west-country alliterative authors who develop the spring description as a prelude to the dream itself: the unknown poet of *Winner and Waster* (c. 1350) for instance, introduces a moral debate with a passage in which some of the features of Langland's opening lines occur, much more elaborately worked. See below, p. 17.

[3] B. Prologue. 214–15 and B. VII. 139.

[4] '. . . I put on rough clothes, as if I were a shepherd . . .'

instead of in the brisker, more pointed manner familiar to us from Chaucer:

> Whan that Aprille with his shoures soote
> The droghte of March hath perced to the roote . . .

Although the two poetic kinds alliterative and non-alliterative, did not exist in complete separation from each other during the mediaeval period,[1] alliterative verse from earliest times was always strongly individual, even idiosyncratic by nature. The 'alliterative way' had its own distinctive poetic art long before the Normans came to England: behind *Piers Plowman* and similar contemporary work, lies a long tradition of poetry obeying aesthetic laws formulated far back in a Germanic past. The alliterative poet of the Middle English centuries works with changed materials, and under many different influences, but the salient features of this verse as it first appears in the Old English period remain constant for Langland's century too.

Common to both is a metrical line of great flexibility: with no fixed syllabic content, and free of rhyme, the alliterative metre of any period is well described as

> . . . a sort of talking style . . . susceptible of literary and artistic subtlety when used professionally and by . . . a trained hand.[2]

The ease with which alliterative poets can range from terse, dramatic, conversational effects to those of great rhetorical splendour is due, primarily, to the nature of this basic metrical form: a line which, by the fourteenth century, takes any number of emphatic accents, ranging from three to six, and is given definition simply by alliteration, and the strong mid-line pause.[3] The best alliterative poets avail themselves of such license to move rapidly between extremes of style; they can be both more casual and more elaborate in a short space than poets of the non-alliterative tradition. The

---

[1] For discussion of the nature and cultural setting of medieval alliterative poetry, see E. Salter, 'The Alliterative Revival,' *M.P.*, LXIV, nos. 2 and 3 (1966, 1967).

[2] P. F. Baum, 'The Meter of the *Beowulf*', *M.P.*, XLVI (1948), p. 76.

[3] The Old English alliterative line respects, as a general rule, four main stresses, three of which are reinforced by alliteration: 'Strǣt wæs stanfah, stig wisode' ('the path was stone-paved, the way stretched ahead') (*Beowulf*, ed. F. Klaeber, London, 1936, *l.* 320) and is composed quantitatively as well as accentually. The development of English from an inflected to an analytic language—a process practically complete by 1400—is one of the basic factors responsible for the change apparent in a line such as 'Wrothe wynde of þe welkyn wrastelez with þe sunne' ('the angry wind of the heavens wrestles against the sun') *Sir Gawain and the Green Knight*, ed. J. R. R. Tolkien and E. V. Gordon, 2nd. ed. rev. N. Davis (Oxford, 1968), *l.* 525

dramatic juxtaposition of formality—sometimes deliberate arti-
ficiality—with naturalness is one of the chief defining characteristics
of alliterative composition. It is not surprising, therefore, to find
the author of a late fourteenth-century verse homily, *Patience*,[1]
passing unselfconsciously from the most brusque of phrasing in
the account of Jonah swallowed by the whale:

> . . . stod up in his stomak that stank as the devel . . .
>
> *(l. 274)*

to the most dignified of oratorical style:

> 'Dewoyde now þy vengaunce, þurȝ vertu of rauthe;
> Þaȝ I be gulty of gyle as gaule of prophetes,[2]
> Þou art god, and alle gowdeȝ ar graythely þyn owen . . .'
>
> *(ll. 284–6)*

Such contrasts are common in the work of these poets. It is, however, when they choose to deal in rich modes of expression that the
essential differences between them and non-alliterative writers are
particularly clear: they are impelled towards verse of an accumulative and palpable splendour unrivalled by the latter:

> Armede hym in a actone with orfraeez fulle ryche . . .
> Aboven that a jesseraunt of jentylle maylez,[3]
> A jupone[4] of Jerodyne jaggede in schredez . . .
>
> *(ll. 902, 905–6)*

These lines, describing the arming of King Arthur, are taken from
an alliterative poem[5] which is lavish with visual image and rich
sound, whether the subject is feasting, armour, clothes or warfare
on land and sea:

> Be than cogge appone cogge, krayers and other,
> Castys crepers one crosse, als to the crafte langes:[6]
> Thane was hede-rapys hewen, that helde upe the mastes;
> Thare was conteke full kene, and crachynge of schippys![7]
> Grett cogges of kampe[8] crasseches in sondyre!
>
> *(ll. 3666–70)*

The taste for overt rhetoric of a declamatory and descriptive sort
was no doubt partly inherited by Middle English alliterative poets.
Old English poetry manipulates words into ornate patterns almost

---

[1] Ed. H. Bateson (Manchester, 1918).
[2] '. . . Though I am guilty of guile—the disgrace of prophets . . .'
[3] '. . . Armed himself in a tunic with rich gold embroideries, above that a coat of elaborate chain-mail . . .'
[4] '. . . a surcoat . . .'
[5] *Morte Arthure*, ed. J. Finlayson (York Medieval Texts, 1967). Long extracts from the poem are presented.
[6] '. . . then ship after ship, and all kinds of small vessels, threw grapplings out, in proper (sea) battle style . . .'
[7] '. . . crashing (together) of ships . . .'   [8] '. . . war-ships . . .'

as if they were the jewels and pieces of enamel used so brilliantly by the craftsmen of that period, or sets them to convey, imaginatively and sensuously, the clash of battle, the grim land and seascapes of the northern world.[1] The doctrines of the twelfth- and thirteenth-century manuals on poetic composition, which influenced most mediaeval poets with any pretensions to style,[2] cannot account alone for the lavish decoration and high colour of much alliterative verse of the north and west of England. Many alliterative writers must have learnt from the same textbooks of rhetoric as Chaucer did, but with startlingly different results: whereas Chaucer's characteristic method is the 'acclimatization', or modification of rhetorical devices—art concealing art—,[3] that of the contemporary alliterative poet is exactly the opposite. Like his Old English forbear, he often engages in elaborate and colourful rhetoric for sheer pride of craftsmanship: display, not concealment, preoccupies him.

But although it would be wrong to say, with one writer,[4] that these alliterative poems are 'achievements not of the artificial but of the natural use of language', their use of rhetoric is indeed so exuberant as well as ingenious that even the most conventionally prescribed descriptions are invested with an excitement we miss in their non-alliterative counterparts. The spring openings to some of the poems, for instance, manage to be, at the same time, more elaborate and more sensuous than the Chaucerian type:

> I layde myn hede one ane hill, ane hawthorne be-syde:
> The throstills full throly they threped to-gedire;
> Hipped up heghwalles fro heselis tyll othire;[5]
> Bernacles with thayre billes one barkes thay roungen;
> The jay janglede one heghe, jarmede the foles;[6]
> The bourne full bremly rane the bankes by-twene;
> So ruyde were the roughe stremys, and raughten so heghe,
> That it was neghande nyghte or I nappe myghte,
> For dyn of the depe watir and dadillyng[7] of fewyllys.
>   (*Winner and Waster*, *ll.* 36–44)[8]

---

[1] Two lively introductory essays on Old English poetry can be found in *Anglo-Saxon Poetry* (Oxford, 1943) by Gavin Bone, and in *Beowulf* (Aldington, 1952) by Edwin Morgan: both are prefaces to translations.

[2] An acquaintance with these manuals can be made, in the first instance, from J. W. H. Atkins, *English Literary Criticism; the Mediaeval Phase* (Cambridge, 1943), Chapter V and Appendix, in which the *Poetria Nova*, by the Englishman, Geoffrey of Vinsauf (c. 1208), is analysed.

[3] See D. Everett, *Essays on Middle English Literature*, Chapter VII.

[4] J. Speirs, *Mediaeval English Poetry. The Non-Chaucerian Tradition* (London, 1957), p. 31.

[5] 'The throstles quarrelled vigorously among themselves; woodpeckers called to each other from the hazel-trees;'

[6] '. . . the birds sang;'   [7] '. . . chattering . . .'   [8] Ed. I. Gollancz (Oxford, 1930).

It is difficult to say whether we are here meeting actual records of 'seasonal experience', or simply a particularly brilliant 'seasonal rhetoric'. When we come to the most gifted of alliterative poets (apart from Langland), the anonymous author of *Sir Gawain and the Green Knight*,[1] we find him equally exhilarated, it seems, by words and weather:

> Bot wylde wederez of the worlde wakned þeroute,
> Clowdes kesten kenly the colde to the erþe,
> With nyȝe innoghe of þe north, þe naked to tene;[2]
> The snawe snitered ful snart, þat snayþed þe wylde;[3]
> The werbelande wynde wapped fro the hyȝe,
> And drof vche dale ful of dryftes ful grete.

> *(ll. 2000–2005)*

With a few notable exceptions,[4] alliterative poems are expansive and digressive in structure. In an age which favoured the long poem or prose work, they are still remarkable for their length and tendency to retard a thematic or narrative flow by description and comment. Many of their authors must have found encouragement for this in the manuals on poetic style, which treated amplification so fully, and said so little about abbreviation.[5] But it is also significant that as early as the Old English period, the natural movement of the alliterative poem seems to have been away from a formal and ordered plan; heroic narrative and elegiac lament of these pre-Conquest years are often markedly digressive and sometimes non-chronological in sequence, achieving a loose-knit unity which is extremely difficult to define or justify in 'classical' terms. They proceed by building up a wealthy accumulation of separate parts, each part receiving strong artistic emphasis.[6] So many alliterative poems of both periods give the impression of having been planned as a loosely-strung collection of episodes rather than as a modulated and disciplined whole that we must

---

[1] The poem exists in one manuscript only (Cotton Nero A.x., in the British Museum) which also contains three other alliterative works—*Pearl* (a dream allegory) *Patience* and *Cleanness* (verse homilies). It is now generally accepted that all four are by the same author, and belong to the later fourteenth century.

[2] '. . . with plenty of north-wind, to torment the naked;'

[3] '. . . biting into wild creatures most cruelly.'

[4] *Sir Gawain and the Green Knight* is firmly and compactly shaped: see the Introduction to the Tolkien and Gordon edition.

[5] See, for instance, the relevant sections in Vinsauf's *Poetria Nova*, analysed by Atkins, *op. cit.*, above.

[6] This can be observed in the greatest heroic poem of that period, *Beowulf*, or in the elegiac laments, *Wanderer* and *Seafarer*. The aesthetic of Anglo-Saxon and Celtic art—illumination and sculpture—has been commented upon similarly: see A. Grabar and C. Nordenfalk, *Early Mediaeval Painting* (Skira, 1957), pp. 109 foll.

inquire whether the authors are working to a special conception of artistic unity; this may not be simply careless aberration from classical principles of composition. A delaying, leisurely pattern in which the interest of the individual part is clearly accepted as sufficient compensation for lack of overall balance and cohesiveness—this description fits alliterative romances and homilies such as the *Morte Arthure*, the *Alexander* poems, the *Gawain* poet's (probable) first work, *Cleanness*,[1] and leads us on naturally to *Piers Plowman*.

The affinities of *Piers Plowman* with this literature are obvious. It has, for example, the wide range of rhythmical variation which is characteristic of alliterative writing. Langland exploits to the full the rhythmical potentiality of the accentual line. From the sleepy movement of the opening lines:

> In a somer seson. whan soft was the sonne . . .

he passes rapidly to the angry staccato of

> Bidders and beggeres. fast aboute ȝede,
> With her belies and her bagges. of bred ful ycrammed;
> Fayteden for here fode[2]. fouȝten atte ale . . .
>
> (B.Prol.40–2)

He is equally competent with the slow ceremonial of high sermon style:

> For, bi hym that me made. miȝte neuere pouerte,
> Miseise, ne myschief. ne man with his tonge,
> Colde, ne care. ne compaignye of theues,
> Ne noither hete ne haille. ne non helle pouke,[3]
> Ne noither fuire ne flode. ne fere of thine enemy,
> Tene the eny tyme. and thow take it with the;
>   *Caritas nichil timet!*
>
> (B.XIII.158–63)

as he is with that of high drama:

> A voice loude in that liȝte. to Lucifer cryeth,
> 'Prynces of this place. unpynneth and unloketh . . .'
>
> (B.XVIII.260–1)

And the authentic accounts of conversation

> 'Ye, bawe!' quod a brewere. 'I wil nouȝt be reuled . . .'
>
> (B.XIX.394)

come easily to his verse.

---

[1] For comment on the structure and style of all these works, see D. Everett, *op. cit.*, Chapter III, 'The Alliterative Revival'.
[2] '. . . begged for their food . . .'   [3] '. . . nor any fiend of hell . . .'

When the occasion demands it, he can draw, as well as any of these poets, upon the latent sensuous power of the alliterative line: the dark onslaught of Antichrist:

> Deth cam dryuende after.and al to doust passhed
> Kynges and kny3tes . . .
>
> (B.XX.99–100)

the horror of Gluttony:

> His guttis gunne to gothely[1].as two gredy sowes . . .
>
> (B.V.347)

the gleam of bribery:

> Coupes of clene golde.and coppis of siluer,
> Rynges with rubis.and richesses manye . . .
>
> (B.III. 22–3)

are strikingly, even oppressively, felt and visualized. Though he allows himself practically no scope for the type of landscape description that most of the alliterative poets love[2] he writes sharply and movingly about *life lived* in the country; the men and women he pities—the 'poure folke in cotes'—get to know the winter world and the elements at closer quarters than the questing knight of romance, and his verse tells us of this with uncomfortable exactness:

> 'Conforte tho creatures.that moche care suffren
> Thorw derth, thorw drouth.alle her dayes here,
> Wo in wynter tymes.for wantyng of clothes,
> And in somer tyme selde.soupen to the fulle . . .'
>
> (B.XIV.175–8)

> Frydayes and fastyng-dayes.a ferthyng-worth of muscles
> Were a feste for suche folke.other so fele cockes . . .[3]
>
> (C.X.94–5)

The length, the digressiveness, the apparent abrupt, episodic quality of *Piers Plowman* are all features which, as we have seen, are to be expected from an alliterative work. Langland seems to indulge freely in expansions and illustrations of all kinds; the extent to which he allows his taste for such things to govern the general movement of the poem reminds us much more of the long alliterative romances and homilies than of a poem such as *Troilus and*

---

[1] '. . . his guts began to rumble . . .'
[2] It is notable that, as the poem continues, the passages introducing successive dreams lose even the small 'landscape-element' we can observe in the opening lines—an indication of the increasing urgency of the poet's visions.
[3] '. . . . or the same amount of cockles . . .'

Criseyde, for instance. And so far it can be said that *Piers Plowman* has much in common with the 'alliterative school'. But the differences are equally important.

At no point does Langland show an interest in the elaborate forms of alliterative verse so intensively and lovingly cultivated by other poets. The open delight in 'art for art's sake', which must explain the high rhetoric to be found in nearly all alliterative poems, is no part of Langland's attitude to his craft. The use of words as if they were jewels:

> His cote wyth þe conysaunce of þe clere werkez
> Ennurned vpon veluet, vertuus stonez
> Aboute beten and bounden, enbrauded semez,
> And fayre furred withinne wyth fayre pelures . . .[1]
>   (*Sir Gawain, ll.* 2026–9)

thick-textured alliteration, sonorous language, often liberally supplied with exotic, colourful terminology—none of this is characteristic of *Piers Plowman*. The 'stock' half-line or conventional alliterative phrase can occasionally be found, but clearly Langland does not draw upon the special poetic diction which most of these writers favoured. For a good deal of the time the alliterative element in his verse is unobtrusive; never as prominent as others make it:

> The schafte schoderede and schotte in the schire beryn,[2]
> That the schadande blode over his schanke rynnys,
> And schewede one his schynbawde, that was schire burneste.[3]
> And so they schyfte and schove, he schotte to the erthe;
>   (*Morte Arthure, ll.* 3844–7)[4]

it is present often in a considerably reduced form:

> 'Ich am a mynstral,' quath this man. 'my name is *Activa-uita*,
> Peers prentys the Plouhman. alle peuple to comfortye.'
> 'What manere mynstralcie. my dere frend,' quath Conscience,
> 'Hast thou vsed other haunted. al thy lyf-tyme?'
>   (C.XVI.194–7)

Although Langland proves that he knows how to load the line—especially for satiric purposes[5]—his general practice is to refuse

---

[1] '. . . his coat-armour with (heraldic) devices in brilliant embroidery, set upon velvet, decorated and adorned with precious stones, embroidered borders, and sumptuously lined inside with expensive furs . . .'
[2] '. . . into the famous warrior . . .'
[3] '. . . and splashed onto his shin-plate, which was burnished brightly.'
[4] This is taken from the description of Sir Gawain attacking the traitor Mordred.
[5] See below, p. 38.

alliteration the dominance it so often has in other contemporary works. The insistent alliteration of the opening lines to *Piers Plowman* is, in this sense, unrepresentative: we shall meet it again in the poem, but always on occasions of heightened importance. The norm is something far less emphatic.

Moreover, having conceded that in structure and procedure this poem is more like alliterative compositions than anything of Chaucer's, for instance, we are forced, on closer acquaintance, to go one stage further, and admit that in certain structural respects it is unique. Episodic and expansive though they may be, other alliterative poems do not prepare us exactly for what we find in *Piers Plowman*. No other poem of the alliterative tradition combines so distinctively rational procedure (in the verse paragraph, the individual speech or episode) with what appears, at first, to be a larger irrationality—an almost inconsequential attitude to the problems of developing and sustaining actions and arguments. The constant interruption of closely-reasoned, well-ordered writing by abrupt changes of thematic direction, and by unheralded entries or departures of allegorical personages is an inescapable part of the experience of reading *Piers Plowman*: we cannot help feeling that Langland often depends upon happy chance for the larger handling of his material. And yet, for all this, we are somehow persuaded that he has total, if loose-reined, control of the poem—we are never reduced to believing, even at moments of greatest complication, that nothing lies beyond what seems dislocated or tangential. By various means, Langland ensures that the dramatic perplexity in which so many of his characters find themselves, is not shared to the same degree by his readers. If, then, in form and methods of procedure, *Piers Plowman* is a much more complex proposition than other alliterative works, and in diction is on the whole simpler, more prosaic,[1] what can we believe guided Langland for the shape and language of his poem?

As far as diction is concerned, it is proper to recall that the highest development of ornate alliterative language did not take place in the poetry of that area from which Langland is usually supposed to have come. If he left the south-west Midlands sometime in the thirteen-fifties to settle henceforth in London, he might have known nothing of the richer alliterative styles that were already

---

[1] This is not to deny that *Piers Plowman* has a high proportion of French-based vocabulary, and uses Latinate theological and philosophical terms: it is 'simpler' in the sense that it avoids the elaborate poetic vocabulary of the alliterative school.

to be found in poems of the more northerly western areas. In *Winner and Waster*, the debate poem of *c.* 1350, lavish alliteration is being used with practised confidence,[1] and to this the sumptuous writing of later fourteenth-century poets from the north-west Midlands—the author of *Sir Gawain*, for instance—is the mature conclusion.

In Langland's part of the west country, however, alliterative verse seems always to have remained fairly unsophisticated. Our earliest example of a large-scale Middle English alliterative work, the chronicle-poem *Brut*,[2] comes from Worcestershire at about 1200; although its author, the priest Layamon, makes a vigorous use of the old alliterative measure, he could not be described as a poet of high and conscious artistry. For the next hundred and fifty years, there is an almost total lack of evidence about the fate of alliterative poetry, but when it does emerge again, in the mid-fourteenth century, the position is basically the same for this area. From the romance, *William of Palerne*,[3] to the later poem on the evils of Richard the Second's reign, *Mum and the Sothsegger*,[4] there is no great increase in elaborate stylishness. The working experience Langland took with him to London would probably have been gained from poetry of this kind, which may still have been in fairly close relationship with popular oral tradition.

In any case, even if he had been familiar with and practised in the most extreme forms of alliterative rhetoric, it is hardly likely that he would have used them in a poem designed to reach not a small courtly audience, but the widest kind of public.[5] Audiences in any part of England except the west and north-west Midlands could not have been expected to appreciate the special conventions of alliterative diction as they were developed in the second half of the fourteenth century—perhaps in response to aristocratic patronage.[6] Unlike the alliterative poet writing at home, in the west, for a known castle or monastic audience, Langland could not assume a community of taste in such matters.

Both factors are probably influential. But when we leave diction and come to the question of the distinctive form of *Piers Plowman*,

---

[1] See above, p. 17.   [2] Ed. F. Madden (London, 1847), 3 vols.
[3] Translated from the French, about 1350, by order of Humphrey de Bohun, Duke of Hereford, ed. W. W. Skeat (E.E.T.S., E.S.1, 1867).
[4] Ed. M. Day and R. Steele (E.E.T.S., O.S. 199, 1936).
[5] See J. A. Burrow, 'The Audience of *Piers Plowman*', *Anglia*, Band 75 (1957).
[6] For a controversial presentation of this theory, see J. R. Hulbert, 'A Hypothesis concerning the Alliterative Revival', *M.P.*, XXVIII (1931), and for a more scholarly approach, C. A. Luttrell, 'Three North West Midland Manuscripts', *Neophilologus* (January 1958).

no immediate explanation is forthcoming and we are entitled to wonder whether we have yet reached the proper ground from which to argue both the nature and the status of Langland's art. *Piers Plowman* cannot be accounted for adequately in terms of ordinary mediaeval poetics, nor in those of the 'alliterative tradition' alone. We must look deeper for the forces at work shaping the poem.

(ii) *The Sermon: theory and practice*

For Langland and his public *Piers Plowman* fulfilled a primarily religious function.[1] This is, in a very real sense, 'applied' not 'pure' art. But having conceded this, we need not go on to assume that a lower standard of achievement will inevitably be expected from such a work. Here, as in the mediaeval sermon, we shall find eloquence—'l'éloquence religieuse où l'Esprit Saint lui-même doit être l'inspirateur'[2]—and it is useful to recall a recent statement on the relationship of religion and art:

> When religious imagination is the dominant force in society, art is scarcely separable from it; for a great wealth of actual emotion attends religious experience, and unspoiled, unjaded minds wrestle joyfully for its objective expression, and are carried beyond the occasion that launched their efforts, to pursue the furthest possibilities of the expressions they have found.[3]

If in one sense religious art is limited, in another it has no bounds; the demands which devotion makes of words and rhythms, or of paint, stone, metal, are more likely, in a period of strong religious activity, to lead in the direction of powerfully expressive work than to inhibit and discourage artists. If *Hymns Ancient and Modern* are not great art forms, the *Stabat Mater* and the *Wilton Diptych* are.

No 'ars poetica' was specifically formulated during the mediaeval period for religious poets such as Langland. But some theoretical discussion of the principles to which vernacular religious literature was produced in the Middle Ages can be found, and this bears relevantly upon *Piers Plowman*. The Prefaces of the translators of Latin devotional works into English contain important basic material, and so do the manuals of instruction on sermon composition. Mediaeval translators preserve a remarkable degree of

---

[1] It is interesting that the earliest version of the poem, the A text, is found in the fourteenth-century 'Vernon' manuscript, in company with devotional prose treatises clearly meant for ecclesiastical use. See M. S. Serjeantson, 'The Index of the Vernon Manuscript', *M.L.R.* XXXII (1937).   [2] Th. Charland, O.P., *Artes Praedicandi* (Paris, 1936), p. 8.
[3] S. Langer, *op. cit.*, p. 402.

uniformity in statements about the aims and nature of their work.[1]
The fact that their labour was, initially and consistently, sacred,
was never forgotten; the point of making vernacular versions of
Latin texts was to render vital doctrine more accessible, and intelligibility was the first concern. But all agree that some quantity of
adornment serves communication well—it can often ensure that
communication is established. In these Prefaces and in the translated
prose itself we can see that the desire to be understood does not
force the translator to reject the ornamentation of his original
completely, but teaches him to turn it to practical ends. In fact,
ornament reinforces sense. The theory and practice of these men
illustrate how natural and fruitful a reconciliation between religion
and art can be; far from impoverishing literature, religion helped
to shape a law of stylistic moderation which had the happiest
results in literary form. In this indissoluble blend of utility and
elegance, the catalyst was the sacred intent of the author, whose
activity was dedicated to God: one translator writes

. . . to the honour of God and of all seyntis than wil we begynne this tretys,[2]

To compare the firm statements made by another[3] in his Preface
with the prose written to such principles is instructive; it becomes
clear that his general problem—although not the special application
of it as a translator—is Langland's too: how to adjust 'sentence'
and art. The book is 'for the edyfycacyon of you that fele symplely
in your owne wyttes and loue to be enformyd'. The Latin will be
freely dealt with where it is difficult: 'y expounde yt and declare yt
more openly'. All must be 'turnyd as the sentence may best be
understondyd', yet he stresses that a balance must be kept between
the right of the sacred text to remain intact, and the natural demands
of the English language:

. . . I laboure to kepe bothe the wordes and the sentence in this boke as farre as
oure language wyll well assente . . .[4]

---

[1] From the early Prefaces of Old English translators such as Alfred the Great and Aelfric
to the far more numerous Middle English examples—those of Richard Rolle, John Purvey,
Nicholas Love and many anonymous writers. See F. Amos, *Early Theories of Translation*
(New York, 1920).

[2] John Capgrave, *Life of St. Gilbert*, ed. J. Munro (E.E.T.S., O.S. 140, 1910).

[3] Dr. Thomas Gascoigne, who made an English version of Divine Service for the Nuns of
Syon before 1450 and called it *The Myroure of our Ladye* (ed. J. H. Blunt, E.E.T.S., O.S. 19,
1873).

[4] *Op. cit.*, pp. 6–7.
The same author, writing of sermon style, has this to say: 'a fanciful method of speaking
hinders perception of the matter to be grasped, and does not manifest the truth, as it is
manifested in plain words and good modes of speech . . .' See G. R. Owst, *Preaching in
Mediæval England* (Cambridge, 1926), p. 311.

C

What he actually achieves within these 'limits' is admittedly close to the Latin, clear of sense and idiomatic, but it is also, like much of Langland's verse, impressively cadenced:

> For God ys a greate Lorde, and a greate Kynge above all goddes. For the same Lord shall not forsake ne caste from hym hys people. For in his hande and power ar all the contrees of erthe. And the hyghnesse and depnesse of mounteyns he beholdeth.
>
> For the see ys hys, and he made yt. And the drye erthe hys handes have grounded.
>
> Come ye and worshyp we, and falle we downe before God. Wepe we before oure Lord that made us.
>
> For he ys our Lord God. For we are hys people, and the sheepe of hys pasture.[1]

Nicholas Love, Prior of the Carthusian House of Mount Grace in Yorkshire, states firmly in the Preface to his *Mirror of the Blessed Life of Jesu Christ*[2] that his dealings with the Latin original are shaped 'as it semeth to the writere hereof most spedeful and edifienge to hem that ben of symple vnderstondynge'.[3] This primarily religious direction of activity ensures a lucid text, but also warmly encourages eloquence at appropriate (religious) moments:

> Why folwe we not after the? Why lowe we not and meke not oure self? Why loue we and holde we and coueite we so besily worschippes and pompes and vanytees of the worlde? Sothely for oure rewme is of this world and for we knowe not oure selfe here as pilgrimes and straungeres . . .[4]

We can, however, come closer to the theory of Langland's art than we do here. In a significant passage from Passus XI, he mentions 'retoryke'; the dreamer is being encouraged to speak out about sin 'in rhetoric':

> 'Thinge that al the worlde wote.wherfore shuldestow spare
> To reden it in retoryke.to arate dedly synne?'[5]
>
> (B.XI.97–8)

This is a clear reference to pulpit rhetoric, the art of preaching, about which so many manuals were written in the Middle Ages. If Langland was familiar with any treatise on style, it would most probably have been of this kind, dealing with the 'ars praedicandi', the art of preaching, and not with the 'ars poetica' such as that which Chaucer is known to have used.[6] There are numerous formal

---

[1] *Op. cit.*, pp. 85–7.   [2] Translated about 1409; ed. L. F. Powell (Oxford, 1908).
[3] *Op. cit.*, p. 8.   [4] *Op. cit.*, p. 86.
[5] 'Why should you hesitate to speak out, eloquently, about something everyone knows to be true, so that deadly sin can be soundly rated?'
[6] The three branches of rhetoric dealt with in the text-books of the twelfth and thirteenth centuries, were the *Ars Poetica*, the *Ars Praedicandi* and the *Ars Dictaminis* (the art of letter-writing).

connections between Piers Plowman and homiletic literature,[1] and
it is at least possible that the manuals of sermon composition may
tell us important things about the nature of Langland's art. In these
manuals, which were designed to help preachers in both Latin and
the vernacular to set out and develop their themes, the basic problems
of the religious artist are most fully debated.[2] Sacred material,
drawn by the preacher out of his texts, must teach, move, and also,
perhaps, delight. Now the old Ciceronian triple aim of rhetoric—
'docere, movere, delectare'—is set into a new context, and new
difficulties arise: how far can the effort of the preacher be directed
lawfully towards delighting by the arts of language and rhythm,
how can peace be made between beauty and usefulness? How also
can a balance be kept between the claims of full edification and
those of unity and consistency in the preacher's main business—
the exhaustive inquiry into his chosen theme? The mediaeval
Artes Poeticae could give little help here; those who consulted them
may have been interested in propriety—the suiting of style to subject
matter—but there were no moral issues at stake. In their lengthy
treatment of how to expand a chosen poetic subject, and of how
to compose as elegantly as possible, they do not cater for the most
urgent needs of the devotional writer, for they have no moral
points of reference. It is in the *Artes Praedicandi* that we find direct
comment on what must have been the preoccupations of most
mediaeval religious artists. Now Langland tells us, at one stage,
of these preoccupations. In Passus XII of the B text the allegorical
figure Imagynatyf accuses him of writing poetry when he might
have been saying prayers:

'And thow medlest the with makynges[3].and my3test go sey thi sauter,
And bidde for hem that 3iveth the bred.for there ar bokes ynowe
To telle men what Dowel is.Dobet, and Dobet bothe,
And prechoures to preue what it is.of many a peyre freres.'
(B.XII.15–18)

---

[1] Many of these are set out by Professor Owst in *Literature and Pulpit in Mediaeval England*,
Chapter IX. The allegorical characters in the poem are often openly preaching: Scripture
(B.XI.103) 'skipte an heigh, and preched', Reason (B.V.11) 'gan arrayen hym.alle the reume
to preche . . .' and the poet himself, as in B.VII.59, often turns from exposition to direct
sermonizing with a particular audience in view—
3e legistres and lawyeres.holdeth this for treuthe . . .
See also B.VI.322 amd B.VII.181.
[2] See Owst, *Preaching in Mediæval England*, Chapter VII, 'Manuals and Treatises'.
Two preaching tracts are printed by Th. Charland, O.P., *op. cit.*; E. Gilson in *Les Idées et
les Lettres* (Paris, 1932), discusses the sermon technique of one preacher, Michel Menot, with
valuable generalizations on religious art.
[3] 'And you play about, writing poetry . . .'

As we learn to expect from Langland, his answer is not simple and decisive—the defence he offers is honestly thoughtful: making poetry is a pleasure, and this is not necessarily harmful, for one may thereby achieve greater aims in the end. Moreover the answers to the questions that trouble him must be pursued through his poetry—if this search of his were not so urgent, and if it seemed that anyone could reveal to him what he seeks, he would devote himself actively to a life of prayer.[1]

Certain things are to be noted here. Langland's basic assumption is that a life of holiness is the highest good, and that prayer is superior not only to the writing of verse, but also to any other activity. This assumption he shares with all serious thinkers of his age; if challenged any poet would have made the same answer: devotion is higher than literature—it is, in fact, of ultimate importance. Secondly, Langland attaches an extreme importance to his particular work; though it is less worthy by nature than prayer, nevertheless it *is* a dedicated task—it is the pursuit of Truth. Thirdly, the delight he takes in his 'makynges' effectively disproves the contention of many critics that Langland was uninterested in the *craft* of poetry. On the other hand, he makes it clear that his pleasure has to be justified by its larger usefulness, because the work on hand is holy. Langland raises issues in these lines which are not raised by Chaucer, for instance, setting out upon the writing of *Troilus and Criseyde* or the *Canterbury Tales*. But they are the same issues faced by mediaeval religious lyrists, homilists, and allegorists.

It is worth stressing that later distinctions between what is artistically satisfying, 'beautiful', and what is expedient in certain circumstances, are sharper than those which were recognized in the Middle Ages. Beauty, in the mediaeval view, was the fulfilment of a set or required conditions, and, in this sense, a grotesque description of a person or place can be 'beautiful'. In this sense, too, a sermon or poem or translation which is not entirely free to avail itself of all the artistic devices known to the writer can be 'beautiful', for it possesses

. . . la beauté de la chose qui est exactement ce qu'elle doit être et satisfait . . . sa propre définition.[2]

The mediaeval religious poet or preacher or translator, while he was certainly conscious of the delicate nature of his task—this maintaining of a balance between the aims of 'docere' and

---

[1] B.XII. 21–9.   [2] E. Gilson, *op. cit.*, p. 119.

'delectare'—did not feel himself constricted to the degree we may imagine. If there can be no 'art for art's sake' in such situations, yet art is called upon to do much; there is the other, perhaps most important aim of religious art—to move: 'toucher, c'est remporter la victoire.'[1]

The preaching manuals are very clear on these points:

... for just as beauty is no help to the pilot in overcoming the dangers of naviga-tion, so over-elegance (curiositas) is no help towards the correction of vice in the sinner.[2]

Robert of Melun writes strongly against the 'inanis suavitas ver-borum' which hides the rich life of the content.[3] And most of the authors are concerned about the proper use of the 'figura verborum', the verbal devices which take up so much space in the Artes Poeticae.[4] They must not be indulged simply as adornments, and their frequency must be checked. On the other hand, there is plenty of evidence to show that certain of these word-devices were considered necessary to the art of preaching. In particular, rhyme, rhythmical phrasing, repetition (in simple or complex form) and antithesis were recommended—all of them figures which had a double usefulness, underlining sense while increasing the emotional response ('docere' and 'movere'). The whole question is summed up well by Robert of Basevorn: the perfect sermon is a 'dulcis mixtura bonorum',[5] wisdom and eloquence. But some distinctions are made between the kinds of eloquence suitable for popular and learned audiences, for sermons in the vernacular or in Latin. The popular sermon must be less elaborate than the learned in word-play and rhythmical patterning, and, on the positive side, it must contain a greater proportion of 'images sensibles', vivid, familiar illustrations which will make immediate impact.[6]

On the larger question of structure and development the treatises have interesting things to say. The majority of sermons started with a Biblical text, and the effort of the preacher was to extract all possible meaning contained in this text, to expound it precisely and movingly. Clearly here the problem was that of attaining to and then of disciplining the fullness of comment required by the spiritual needs of the congregation. There must be a dominant

[1] Gilson, *op. cit.*, pp. 109–110, quoted from St. Augustine, *De Doctrina Christiana*.
[2] John of Wales, quoted by Gilson, *op. cit.*, p. 99, note I.
[3] Quoted by H. Caplan, 'Classical Rhetoric and the Mediaeval Theory of Preaching', *Classical Philology* XXVIII (1933), p. 82.
[4] See, for instance, the analysis of Vinsauf's treatise on poetic art in Atkins, *op. cit.*, Appendix.
[5] Charland, *op. cit.*, p. 249.   [6] Gilson, *op. cit.*, p. 113.

theme, or themes, but there must also be the most minute and varied support from all kinds of relevant evidence. The theorists liken sermon structure to that of a cathedral, which at first may seem complicated, but reveals, on examination, a simple basic plan.[1] They also draw analogies from musical composition—one theme developed in innumerable variations, each part being essential to the whole. In the full development, the 'opening out' of a text as theme, the sermon-writer is in a somewhat similar position to the secular poet, occupied in the fullest possible amplification of *his* theme or narrative. It might seem that in this both secular and religious theorists will be in agreement. Yet the Artes Praedicandi carefully stress as, of course, the Artes Poeticae, in their great sections on amplification do not, that edification must be the guiding principle in departures from theme and returns to it. Whatever adds decisively to the fruitful understanding of the hearers may be indulged, but not lengthening and beautifying for its own sake.[2] Unity may be considerably helped by the repetitive verbal devices mentioned above; they are best justified when used to pick out, over the length of a sermon, themes and sub-themes.

There is one more point to make. In certain circumstances, when the choice lay plainly between edification and total unity, edification won:

> Magis enim amanda est animarum aedificatio quam sermonis continuatio.[3]

On this principle, the religious enthusiasm of the preacher could lead him to artistic abruptness of discourse, to an accumulation of metaphors and exempla, to disproportionately extensive treatment of one doctrinal point. And we must concede that the mediaeval homilist or religious poet saw a fitting beauty in this, for it was a beauty which sprung from perfect compliance with sacred demands; the work was fulfilling its prescribed nature.

We can, then, find in the prefaces of translators and in the preaching manuals, a body of theory about the writing of religious literature which may help us when it comes to reading and judging the literature itself. If this does not compel us to rate religious prose and poetry higher than we have done before, it certainly asks us, in our descriptions, to use terms different from those of ordinary literary criticism, or, at least, to use them in a different way. For this law which lies at the back of religious meditation,

---

[1] E. de Bruyne, *Études d'Esthétique Médiévale* (Brugge, 1946) 'comme la cathédrale, il se révèle, à l'analyse, d'une facture extrêmement simple', II.59.
[2] Gilson, *op. cit.*, p. 149.   [3] Quoted by Gilson, *op. cit.*, p. 143.

lyric, sermon or allegory, presses beauty into the service of usefulness, engages ornament for the labour of sense; it subordinates 'fine-writing' to intelligibility—sometimes dispensing with it entirely, sometimes employing it most fully for a particular end. It requires that the shape and movement of a work should follow a devotional pattern; tempo and emphases may, therefore, be slightly unfamiliar compared with those of secular art. Surprising changes of direction and digression may also be justified within these terms which lay such stress upon 'aedificatio'. But if the religious purpose controls, it also encourages, gives the artist great scope for the exercise of his skills and imagination. In practice the devotional pattern is often the best possible guide for the literary pattern; devotional needs can draw out the finest art. And we should now see how all this applies to the 'poetic art' in *Piers Plowman*.

Only a very prejudiced reader could fail to be persuaded that Langland does not consistently—nor, I believe, fundamentally— feel the need to communicate as a poet; the pressure of the need to be understood comes through most urgently, but it is as a man of spirituality, with truths and experiences of truths to commit to others that he wishes to become fully articulate. Two examples may show, in a preliminary fashion, how the driving force, the real centre of energy in his work is spiritual, and how poetry serves this dedication. The first is drawn from Passus V, at the moment when Piers tells the crowd of repentant pilgrims how they can reach the Court of St. Truth, or God. This is one of the most important and delicate episodes in the whole of the first section of the poem. Piers is saying to the pilgrims that this 'road to St. Truth' along which they are all so eager to travel, is circular—it ends in their own hearts. The search for God brings the traveller back to find God within. And there is more to the passage than this—it is a point of departure not only for these pilgrims, but for Piers also. What he forecasts for them, happens to him; the search for Truth ends, miraculously, in him, as by successive transformations he becomes what was sought. Here, in this Passus, is a significant summing up of previous teaching, and a signpost to future events; it is a decisive stage in the poem's development.[1] Clarity is essential, and Langland, driving himself towards intelligibility, and not necessarily towards poetry, has treated his subject matter in verse which is straightforward enough, but by no means beautiful. The allegory is kept simple; it is a spiritual geography such as a

[1] See below, pp. 97 foll.

child could understand—and this in itself is a virtue, for the pilgrims who stand listening to Piers have become 'as a little child' so that they may be received into the kingdom of Heaven. They are told patiently of the countryside of the ten commandments, which surrounds the court of God:

'And so boweth forth by a broke. Beth-buxum-of speche,
Tyl ȝe fynden a forth. ȝowre-fadres-honoureth,
  Honora patrem et matrem, etc.
Wadeth in that water. and wascheth ȝow wel there,
And ȝe shul lepe the liȝtloker. al ȝowre lyf-tyme.
And so shaltow se Swere-nouȝte-. but-if-it-be-for-nede-
And-namelich-an-ydel-. the-name-of-god-almyȝti.
Thanne shaltow come by a crofte. but come thow nouȝte there-inne;
That crofte hat[1] Couetye-nouȝte-. mennes-catel-ne-her-wyues-
Ne-none-of-her-serauntes-. that-noyen-hem-myȝte;
Loke ȝe breke no bowes there. but if it be ȝowre owne.
Two stokkes there stondeth. ac stynte ȝe nouȝte there,
They hatte Stele-nouȝte, Ne-slee-nouȝte. stryke forth by bothe;
And leue hem on thi left halfe. and loke nouȝte thereafter;
And holde wel thyne haliday. heighe til euen.
Thanne shaltow blenche at a berghe. Bere-no-false-witnesse,
He is frithed in with floreines. and other fees many;[2]
Loke thow plukke no plante there. for peril of thi soule.
Thanne shal ȝe se Sey-soth-. so-it-be-to-done-
In-no-manere-ellis-nauȝte-. for no-mannes-biddynge.'
                                                    (B.V. 575-593)

The court itself is described minutely—its buttresses of Belief, its roof leaded with Love, its drawbridge of Prayer, its sentinel of Grace—and now the pilgrims have been brought, hardly realizing it, to the threshold of a mystery. The poetry quickens to express it:

'And if Grace graunte the. to go in this wise,
Thow shalt se in thi-selue. Treuthe sitte in thine herte,
In a cheyne of charyte. as thow a childe were,
To suffre hym and segge nouȝte. aȝein thi sires wille.'
                                                    (B.V. 614-17)

By means of a slow, painstaking approach to a central imaginative statement, Langland has enabled pilgrims (and reader) to accept a mystery unquestioningly, with the faith of a child. The poetry has been reduced—what we are left with sounds like pure fact; it is something given to us on trust, to take further into the maze of the dream, where its meaning will be not only explored, but experienced.

[1] '... is called ...'
[2] 'Then you must turn aside from a hill (called) "Bear-no-false-witness"; it is wooded with florins, and many other sorts of payment;'

There are many occasions such as these, when no honest defence of the writing as poetry can be offered; it *can* be defended, however, on the grounds that its plain intelligibility matters very much to the larger development of the work. Better be accused of dullness than risk obscurity at these points; it is a logic of spiritual, not aesthetic responsibility, such as the sermon theorists would have understood.[1]

Numerous passages of inferior poetry in *Piers Plowman* can be accounted for in this way.[2] There is no bad writing of the exaggerated, showy kind, to which other alliterative poets were drawn. And there is very little bad verse of a highly intellectualized nature; Langland deals with intellectual material, but his constant endeavour is to elucidate and to simplify it. Consequently if his writing is unpoetical on such occasions, it is usually because he over-labours his commentary—he is not obscure, but irritatingly (to modern taste) didactic.

At the other extreme, there are the passages of poetry wholly admirable by modern critical standards, which illustrate not so much how Langland's art improves when he escapes the constricting sense of spiritual responsibility, but rather how closely dependent upon religious ideas and experiences his best art is. The description of Avarice[3] can be called a vivid piece of work in the genre of grotesque realism, but in many ways this is a superficial kind of labelling. The success of this portrait and of the others which make up the cavalcade of the Deadly Sins, cannot be disassociated from Langland's deep spiritual knowledge of the subtle, many-sided, and horrifying nature of sin. They are not to be regarded as brilliant miniatures, separable from the rest of the text, and praised for their surprising anticipation of later dramatic or 'character' literature. They are natural products of a fierce and comprehensive effort to grasp and understand the place of evil in the world.[4] The sharpness

---

[1] Many of the differences between the B and the C versions of the poem can be seen as the result of the working of such logic: in revising his work (assuming Langland's authorship of all three versions) Langland was not afraid to dispense with good poetry if greater clarity could be obtained thereby. See Donaldson, *op. cit.*, Chapter III.

[2] A passage such as C.IV.315 foll., in which Langland illustrates the distinction between reward and bribery by analogies drawn from grammar seems to me to be another case in point. He makes the sense absolutely clear: the language is strong, direct and precise, but it is poetic only in a very limited sense. To praise it as Professor Mitchell does (*op. cit.*, p. 25) for its moving and striking poetic qualities seems to me to be doing Langland a disservice; in this way we misrepresent the nature of his art.   [3] B.V. 188 foll. Quoted above, p. 9.

[4] On the kind of realism we find here, see E. Auerbach, *Mimesis*, tr. W. R. Trask (New York, 1957), pp. 11-12. 'What he (the Biblical writer) produced, then, was not primarily oriented towards "realism" (if he succeeded in being realistic it was merely a means, not an end); it was oriented towards truth.'

of Langland's vision of the Seven Deadly Sins is most closely related
to his sharp vision of the central issue in this divinely paradoxical
situation: man *encumbered* with sin, set aside from God, yet man
fighting with sin, manifesting his finest Christ-inspired qualities.
Sin, therefore, is the cause of man's deepest degradation: it can also
be the occasion of his greatest triumph. The problem which obsessed
contemplatives of Langland's day, such as Dame Julian of Norwich,
and which was answered for her in words both enigmatic and
satisfying,[1] is also Langland's problem:

> 'Now god', quod he, 'that of thi goodnesse.gonne the worlde make,
> And of nauȝte madest auȝte.and man most liche to thi-selue,
> And sithen suffredest for to synne.a sikenesse to vs alle,
> And al for the best, as I bileue.what euere the boke telleth,
> *O felix culpa! O necessarium peccatum Ade!* etc.
> For thourgh that synne thi sone.sent was to this erthe,
> And bicam man of a mayde.mankynde to saue,
> And madest thi-self with thi sone.and vs synful yliche . . .'
> (B.V. 488 foll.)

In sinning and in determining to repent of sin, man is most clearly
God's creation; Christ appeared first, after his Resurrection, to the
once-sinful Mary Magdalene, and only then to his mother:

> '*Non veni vocare iustos, sed peccatores ad penitenciam.*'

Before sin can be corrected, utilized as a powerful means towards
the salvation of man, it must be thoroughly known. And to know it
thoroughly, one must have a strong apprehension of its opposite—
divine goodness. So Langland's meticulous analysis of different
aspects of the disease is made by the light of his convictions about
goodness. It is this which illuminates for him the Rabelaisian, over-
flowing evil of Gluttony, the sleek, savouring evil of Lechery,
the blustering, violent evil of Anger, the threadbare evil of Avarice.
And the necessity of conveying what he sees to others provides him
with urgent motives for poetic composition. In his treatment of
Avarice, for instance, Langland penetrates to the essential meanness
of the creature's besetting sin; every element of sense and sound
in the portrait is calculated to impress the pinched, pared horror
of him—sticky beard, sagging cheeks, louse-ridden hat and cloak.
But this is not simply a literary calculation; words, rhythms have a
a religious inspiration, and a religious function—they serve a spiritual
view of 'starved, ignoble nature', God's image befouled.

---

[1] 'It behoved that there should be sin; but all shall be well, and all shall be well, and all
manner of thing shall be well.' *Revelations of Divine Love*, ed. G. Warrack (London, 1923),
p. 56.

That the poetic quality of *Piers Plowman* is most usefully defined in terms of this 'divine rhetoric', can be illustrated in small and in large. Most critics have commented on the artlessness of his style, and it is true that there is little verbal trickery of a purely decorative kind in the work. The overall effect of a good deal of Langland's verse is that of an almost unbelievable naturalness in vocabulary and rhythm. The traditional tendencies of the alliterative line towards dramatic freedom of phrasing are carried further by Langland than by any other mediaeval poet.[1] Without destroying the essential metrical form of the line, he can produce poetry which is, firmly and directly, 'language really used by men'; here, for instance, this passage, while remaining verse, reads as an angry outburst of speech:

'Ʒe, go thi gate,'[2] quod Pees. 'bi god, for al thy phisyk,
But thow conne somme crafte. thow comest nouʒt her-inne!
I knewe such one ones. nouʒte eighte wynter passed,
Come in thus ycoped. at a courte there I dwelt,
And was my lordes leche. and my ladyes bothe.
And at the last this limitour,[3] . tho my lorde was out,
He salued so owre wommen. til somme were with childe!'
(B.XX.339–345)

Similarly, the dialogue between Gluttony and 'Beton the brewestere' varies formal poetic patterning in the interests of an authentic speech-flow:

Now bigynneth glotoun. for to go to schrifte,
And kaires him to-kirke-ward. his coupe to schewe.[4]
Ac Beton the brewestere. bad hym good morwe,
And axed of hym with that. whiderward he wolde.
'To holi cherche', quod he. 'forto here masse,
And sithen I wil be shryven. and synne namore.'
'I haue gode ale, gossib', quod she. 'Glotown, wiltow assaye?'
'Hastow auʒte in thi purs. any hote spices?'
'I haue peper and piones', quod she. 'and a pounde of garlike,
A ferthyngworth of fenel-seed. for fastyng dayes.'
Thanne goth Glotoun in—
(B.V.304–14)

---

[1] Miss Helen Gardner, in *The Art of T. S. Eliot* (New York, 1950), p. 31, supports her assertion that Langland's metre lacks variety of pace by the opening passages of *Piers Plowman*. But these lines are quiet and regular of rhythm by deliberate design; we cannot expect subtle and various rhythm here, for the words describe a man wandering and falling asleep.
[2] '. . . be on your way . . .'   [3] '. . . begging friar . . .'
[4] '. . . and makes off towards church to confess his sins.'

No modern poet has ever surpassed Langland for his frank dealings with the purely disgusting: fried fish, stale vegetables, filthy clothes, vomit, stench and toothache:

> Ac Glotoun was a gret cherle. and a grym in the liftynge,
> And coughed vp a caudel. in Clementis lappe;
> Is non so hungri hounde. in Hertford schire
> Durst lape of the leuynges. so vnlouely thei smau3te.[1]
>
> (B.V.360-3)

or for conveying the sensuous impact of cold, discomfort, hunger:

> 'And thou3 his glotynye be to gode ale. he goth to cold beddynge,
> And his heued vn-heled. unesiliche i-wrye;[2]
> For when he streyneth hym to streche. the strawe is his schetes;
> So for his glotonie and his grete scleuthe. he hath a grevous penaunce,
> That is welawo whan he waketh. and wepeth for colde.'
>
> (B.XIV.231-4)

Even more impressive is the plainness of his verse when expressing the most profound of mysteries; the sense is deep, yet accessible to all:

> 'For in kynde knowynge in herte. there a my3te bigynneth.
> And that falleth to the fader. that formed vs alle,
> Loked on vs with loue. and lete his sone deye
> Mekely for owre mysdedes. to amende vs alle;'
>
> (B.I.163-6)

These lines, already quoted above (p. 3) for their naturalness to the ear of a modern reader, show us that such naturalness has the closest possible connection with religious motives; like the remarkable simplicity of some mediaeval devotional lyrics and mystical writings, it is the literary manifestation of unquestioning belief, which demands no more and no less of the poet than lucid statement of acceptable and accepted truth. To commend the above lines or these:

> 'Iesu Cryste on a Iewes dou3ter a-ly3te. gentil woman though she were,
> Was a pure pore mayde. and to a pore man wedded.'
>
> (B.XI.240-1)

for their poetic and dramatic simplicity is equivalent to commending the words 'God is love' or 'And after this I saw God in a point'[3] for their artistic qualities only.

---

[1] '... so disgusting they smelt.   [2] '... and his bare head uncomfortably twisted ...'
[3] Dame Julian of Norwich, *op. cit.*, p. 26.

But we should not fail to notice the considerable amount of rhetoric the poem does contain. It occurs in strict agreement with the principle discussed above—never for beautification, or as an end in itself, but always for the further enriching and clarifying of the sense. The more complicated patterns of sound—frequently met in the work of the *Gawain* poet—are unusual in *Piers Plowman*. But many forms of verbal repetition, recommended by the preaching manuals, for instance, are part of Langland's normal practice. It is difficult to decide whether Langland would have thought in terms of 'figures of style' as he wrote, or whether he imitated the practice of others unconsciously. At any rate certain figures are a familiar part of his style. The repetition of a word root with different inflectional endings (adnominatio) occurs in

'No', quod Pacyence paciently,. and out of his poke hente
Vitailles of grete vertues . . .
(B.XIV.36–7)

'Ich lay by the louelokeste[1]. and loued hem neuere after'
(C.VII.192)

'The my3te of goddes mercy . that my3t us alle amende'
(B.XVI.271)

'And tyl prechoures prechyng. be preued on hemseluen . . .'
(B.IV.122)

'Shipmen and shepherdes. that with shipp and shepe wenten'
(B.XV.354)

Play on words of similar sound but different meaning is common:

'Lyf seith that he lyeth. and hath leyde hus lyf to wedde . . .'
(C.XXI.30)

'And gyle in thi gladde chere. and galle is in thi lawghynge.'
(B.XVI.155)

And this is carried to the dramatic lengths of strong antithesis (contentio) in

'At churche in the charnel. cheorles aren vuel to knowe,
Other a knyght fro a knaue. other a queyne fro a queene.'[2]
(C.IX.45–6)

The figure of 'similiter cadens' (balance of words with similar ending) is added to antithesis in

[1] 'I lay beside the loveliest . . .'
[2] 'In the charnel-house at the church it is difficult to pick out who are the peasants—to know a knight from a ruffian or a harlot from a queen.'

'And that that rathest rypeth.roteth most saunest.'[1]

(C.XIII. 222)

Another very characteristic verbal pattern is that of 'commutatio'—the reversal of the order of the first half of the line in the second half:

'By sorcerye som tyme.and som tyme by maistrye.'

(C.VII.191)

'Doctoures of decres.and of diuinite maistres,'

(B.XV.373)

'Ac thi drynke worth deth.and deop helle thy bolle.'

(C.XXI.410).

'Fissch to lyue in the flode.and in the fyre the crykat . . .'

(B.XIV.42)

On the whole, alliteration is moderately used—the 'blocked' style of parts of the *Morte Arthure* or *Sir Gawain* is not representative of Langland.[2] But he can turn out a richly packed line, occasionally adding rhyme:

. . . fresh flesch other fische.fryed other bake,

(B.VI.312)

'I wolde nou3t greue god', quod Piers.'for al the good on grounde . . .'

(B.VI.231)

It is worth pointing out that in their contexts, and in very different ways, both of these lines warrant increased emphasis; the first is a contemptuous reference to pampered labouring classes, who insist on luxurious food, the second is a fervent and rather anxious statement by Piers to Hunger, who has been giving him authoritative but (as it turns out) limited advice on how to deal with the ills of mankind.

As might be expected, however, the best illustration of Langland's use of stylistic devices comes from more extensive passages. There are many instances in *Piers Plowman* of sustained antithetical writing in which half-lines and lines are balanced syntactically and rhythmically against one another (contentio and compar) and the final emphatic stamp given by repetition of the initial word of each line. Accumulative rhetoric such as this, which drives forward relentlessly to produce a crisis of emotion in the listeners, is particularly characteristic of the mediaeval pulpit, and it is from sermon-type passages in *Piers Plowman* that the best examples come. Here, in a

---

[1] 'And whatever ripens earliest, rots soonest.'   [2] See above, pp. 16–18.

fine piece of disciplined oratory, Reason does not spare to 'reden it
in retoryke. to arate dedly synne' :[1]

> 'Rede me nouʒte,' quod Resoun. 'no reuthe to haue
> Til lordes and ladies. louien alle treuthe,
> And haten al harlotrye. to heren it, or to mouthen it;
> Tyl Pernelles purfil. be put in here hucche;[2]
> And childryn cherissyng. be chastyng with ʒerdes;
> And harlotes holynesse. be holden for an hyne;[3]
> Til clerken coueitise be. to clothe the pore and to fede,
> And religious romares. *recordare* in here cloistres,
> As seynt Benet hem bad. Bernarde and Fraunceys;
> And til prechoures prechyng. be preued on hemseluen;
> Tyl the kynges conseille. be the comune profyte;
> Tyl bisschopes baiardes. ben beggeres chambres,[4]
> Here haukes and her houndes. helpe to pore religious;'
>
> (B.IV.113–125)

Even more important in this process of reinforcing sense by
art is the weaving of a key-word into a verse paragraph. Repetition
for emphasis (traductio) is an established 'figure', and Langland's
skilful use of it in the following quotation could serve as a model
for any rhetorician. The word 'meed'[5] falls insistently, yet varies
in position along the verse line:

> 'It bicometh to a kynge. that kepeth a rewme,
> To ʒive *mede* to men. that mekelich hym serueth,
> To alienes and to alle men. to honoure hem with ʒiftes;
> *Mede* maketh hym biloued. and for a man holden.
> Emperoures and erlis. and al manere lordes
> For ʒiftes han ʒonge men. to renne and to ride.
> The pope and alle prelatis. presentz vnderfongen,[6]
> And *medeth* men hem-seluen. to meyntene his lawes.
> Seruauntz for her seruise. we seth wel the sothe,
> Taken *mede* of here maistre. as thei mowe accorde.
> Beggeres for here biddynge. bidden men *mede*;
> Mynstralles for here murthe. *mede* thei aske.
> The kinge hath *mede* of his men. to make pees in londe;
> Men that teche chyldren. craue of hem *mede*.
> Prestis that precheth the poeple. to gode, asken *mede*,
> And masse-pans and here mete. at the mele-tymes.
> Alkynnes crafty men. crauen *mede* for here prentis;
> Marchauntz and *mede*. mote nede go togideres;
> No wiʒte as I wene. withoute *mede* may libbe.'   (B.III.208–226)

---

[1] See above, p. 26.   [2] 'Until Peronelle's fur trimmings are put away in a drawer . . .'
[3] 'And the piety of fools be held in contempt . . .'
[4] 'Until bishops' steeds go to provide houses for beggars.'
[5] 'Meed' can mean either just or false reward (bribery) and Langland is preoccupied in
Passus II and III with an investigation of its double nature. Here Lady Meed (false reward)
justifies herself at court.   [6] '. . . accept presents . . .'

Similarly, the word 'guile' runs through the first part of Christ's speech at the Harrowing of Hell, pointing the dominant theme of the occasion; he is addressing Lucifer—the beguiler outwitted by a far better, a *supreme* plan.[1] Here, however, Langland plays upon the word over a longer period and more elaborately than in the above passage. Satan's first mention of the word 'guile' refers to Lucifer's deception of Eve in the garden of Eden:

> 'For thow gete hem with gyle.and his gardyne breke,'
>
> B.XVIII.284

It is taken up by Gobelyn a few lines later:

> 'For god wil nou3t be bigiled'.quod Gobelyn, 'ne be-iaped' (290)

Then, triumphantly, the word is used by Christ in his refutation of the Devil. The whole movement is that of a gradual crescendo, from the unobtrusive beginning by Satan to Christ's emphatic reiterations:

> 'Thow, Lucyfer, in lyknesse.of a luther addere,[2]
> Getest by *gyle*.tho that god loued;
> And I, in lyknesse of a leode[3].that lorde am of heuene,
> Graciousliche thi *gyle* haue quytte.go *gyle* a3eine *gyle*!
> And as Adam and alle.thorw a tre deyden,
> Adam and alle thorw a tree.shal torne a3eine to lyue;
> And *gyle* is bigyled.and in his *gyle* fallen.'
>
> (B.XVIII.352–57)

This is followed immediately by another verse paragraph studded with repetitions impressing the theme of Christ's divine thirst for man's love. Here it is impossible to think that the patterning is fortuitous, especially since the passage opens with a striking balanced antithesis of words and ideas:

> 'That art doctour of deth.*drynke* that thow madest!
> For I, that am lorde of lyf.loue is my *drynke*,
> And for that *drynke* to-day.I deyde vpon erthe.
> I fau3te so, me *threstes* 3et, for mannes soule sake;
> May no *drynke* me moiste.ne my *thruste* slake,
> Tyl the vendage falle.in the vale of Iosephath,
> That I *drynke* ri3te ripe must.*resureccio mortuorum*,
> And thanne shal I come as a kynge.crouned with angeles,
> And han out of helle.alle mennes soules.'
>
> (B.XVIII.362–370)   )

---

[1] B.XVIII. 332–360.   [2] '. . . in the likeness of a foul adder .
[3] '. . . in man's likeness . . .'

If the verbal artifice of the poem is directed towards the production of a lucid, emphatic text which will both instruct and move, so too is the metaphor. Professor Owst has shown how many of the subjects chosen by Langland for illustration are those of the mediaeval pulpit:[1] the Trinity as a fist (B.XVII.137 foll.) or as a burning taper (B.XVII.203 foll.), of the unreformed soul as a smoky cottage with a chiding wife (B.XVII.315 foll.).

The metaphor is not generally abstruse nor elaborated beyond the strict needs of the matter in hand; serving a simple purpose—that of elucidation—it must possess the same graphic directness as the exemplum of the popular preacher. The demands made by the preaching manuals for vernacular sermons to be rich in 'images sensibles' and material representations easily graspable are well answered by Langland's (apparently) original metaphor: the rose on a thorny stem (A.X.119–121), icicles melting on cottage eaves (B.XVII.226–8), seeds of various kinds (C.XIII.179–192), the mist on hillsides (B.Prol.214), the sharp needle and the thin linden-leaf (B.I. 151–6). The range of subject is interesting, but the use made of the material is absolutely functional. Lengthy development of metaphor only takes place when the theme is of high importance and difficulty, needing some careful 'opening-out' for full comprehension.

In Passus XVII (B text) we have an example of this: the extremely long investigation of the nature of the Trinity by means of the metaphors of fist (palm and fingers) and taper (wax and wick) which takes well over a hundred lines to complete. We might compare with this the compressed and justly admired metaphors in Passus I (B text) explaining the nature of the Incarnation and Divine love—a space of six lines only is sufficient. The difference is not accidental. When Holy Church, in Passus I, is instructing the Dreamer about the direction and nature of the search which is to lead him throughout the poem, she speaks conclusively about essentials. She tells him about Truth, and Love, gives him his points of reference, his goal. It is enough for him, at that moment, to be ordered and inspired; the details and the complexities come later. Therefore the divine paradox of heavenly love which, though full and rich, needed to take on human form before it was perfect, is conveyed in a metaphor—or, rather, a series of metaphors—which *stress* the paradox: fullness, by taking on more, becomes light. It is a somewhat daring procedure, safeguarded by

---

[1] *Literature and Pulpit*, Chapter II.

the fact that the familiarity of the objects used for illustration brings
the paradox within the imaginative compass of the audience:

> 'For heuene myȝte nouȝte holden it.it was so heuy of hym-self,
> Tyl it hadde of the erthe.yeten his fylle,
> And whanne it haued of this folde[1].flesshe and blode taken,
> Was neuere leef vpon lynde.liȝter ther-after,
> And portatyf and persant.as the poynt of a nedle,
> That myȝte non armure it lette.ne none heiȝ walles.'
>
> (B.I.151-6)

By the time Passus XVII has been reached, the situation is quite
different. The dreamer is approaching the supreme vision of the
poem: divine love demonstrated in the person of Piers—Christ,
the paradox Holy Church discussed in Passus I. It is tremendously
important that, before the drama of Christ's Passion begins, the
dreamer should be in fullest command of knowledge about the
spiritual forces at work in that drama, and about his allegiance to
them. His questions at this point, put to the Good Samaritan (a
'type' or prefiguring of Christ) show that he is not quite in
command. He is uncertain whether his paramount duty should be
faith in the Trinity or love of Christ—'owre lorde aboue alle'.
The Good Samaritan resolves this false separation of allegiances:
both are necessary, are dependent on each other. To love Christ
fully he must have faith in the nature and power of the Trinity:
to understand the perfect charity at the centre of the mystery of
the Crucifixion, he must understand the divine wisdom and grace
which are indivisible from it. Moreover he must realize that for
man, in his turn, to fail in charity is so decisive a fall from the
grace of the Holy Spirit as to make his spiritual regeneration well-
nigh impossible. The dreamer must be prepared to receive the events
of the next Passus as timeless action in which the united working of
the Trinity makes the divine purpose abundantly clear. Here, then,
is the proper time for an expansive, detailed investigation; nothing
can be left to chance, and the Good Samaritan explains patiently
to the Dreamer—'yhere now and know it'—by these two long
metaphors, the subtle interaction of faith and love, grace and love,
in the Supreme Being, and in the microcosm, man. We may call
the elaborated metaphors disproportionately long and deliberately
opened-out; they have, however, a special appropriate beauty of
their own, proceeding towards moving conclusions such as this:

[1] '. . . of this earth . . .'

'For euery manere good man.may be likned to a torche,
Or elles to a tapre.to reuerence the trinitee;
And who mortereth a good man.me thynketh, by myn inwyt,
He fordoth the leuest ly3te.that owre lorde loueth.'
(B.XVII.276–9)

and towards the great conclusion of

Crystes passioun and penaunce.
(B.XVIII.6)

But apart from formal metaphor, the poem has a considerable amount of vivid figurative language thrown out almost casually—sometimes only half-developed as metaphor. Langland visualizes the proude who 'to pore peple . han peper in the nose' (B.XV.197) Christ who 'blewe alle thi blissed . in-to the blisse of paradise' (B.V.503). In a perfect world, the hunting parson would hunt only spiritually—'Prestes and persones . with *placebo* to hunte—' (B.III.309) chastity without charity should be 'cheyned in helle' (B.I.186). The pompous doctors of learning 'gnawen god with the gorge . whan her gutte is fulle' (B.X.57), grace 'sholde growe and be grene' (B.XV. 416). Examples could be multiplied—the pictorial element in Langland's imagination is strong, and works almost continuously.

But the strongest proof of Langland's power in the world of metaphor must come, of course, not from this material, but from the work considered as a whole. At its highest, *Piers Plowman* explores the central problems of the universe through metaphor; in allegorical conceptions such as Piers Plowman himself Langland best displays his energy and subtlety. A poem such as this gives simile and metaphor an important but necessarily subordinate rôle to play; as in a homily, they support and illuminate but do not, in themselves, carry the main theme.[1]

For Langland's art cannot be judged properly in isolated quotations. When dealing above with verbal devices and metaphor it has often been necessary to discuss them in a wide context; the difficulty of lifting out portions of the text without weakening or even distorting their real nature and function is considerable. It must be on an extensive, continuous reading that *Piers Plowman* stands or falls in our estimation.[2] In the first twenty lines of the poem,

[1] This relationship of metaphor and theme is one more link between *Piers Plowman* and sermon literature.
[2] Donaldson, *op. cit.*, p. 72, puts this admirably:
'The poem may, incidentally, contain a number of one-line gems, but if we spend our time admiring these, instead of trying to grasp the broad significance, there is something wrong with our perspective.'

Langland announces an undertaking which would test the powers
of any poet to the utmost, and invites us, therefore, to inquire how
he sustained and developed his theme, how his large vision was
shaped to his poetry.

Authoritative studies have been made of the construction of
Piers Plowman—the ways in which the poet co-ordinates his diverse
materials. Theories of formal unity have been proposed, based on
the four divisions indicated in the manuscript headings: Prologue
and Passus I–VII, Passus VIII–XV (Dowel), Passus XVI–XVIII
(Dobet), Passus XIX–XX (Dobest),[1] and on the character and
appearances of Piers the Plowman as a symbolic representation of
the progress of the poem.[2] More recently it has been suggested
that the search for formal unity is a mistaken one. It is 'the poet's
perception of moral values and social principles and his preoccupation with human material which give the poem its unity'.[3] We are
told that the only real unity is imaginative: 'He (Langland) draws
that design conclusively away from a formal into a truly imaginative unity.'[4] The same writer does not think that other mediaeval
literature can help us much to understand what kind of a poem
this is: if it is like any one poetic kind it is 'like that of the genuinely
new "kind" for which the eighteenth century treatise poem paves the
way'.[5] On the one hand we may be encouraged to think that the
design of the work can be deduced fairly easily from the text; on
the other hand, we are left in an uncertain position, with a poem
of few contemporary literary affiliations, whose real cohesiveness
we may insult if we attempt to bring it into any sort of formal
artistic terms. I think that on this question of wholeness and unity
we could be both less and more precise. While it is true that at the
high points of his poem we see 'the preparation is not the creature's
but the Creator's'[6] nevertheless in the general organization of the
work the creature himself, proceeding to fairly well-established
mediaeval, literary and devotional patterns, can be clearly discerned.

We embark upon Piers Plowman, as we do upon a long poem of
any period, with the expectation that it will be uneven of quality;
we may demand that the poet possess the ability to hold our interest
over long stretches of the work, but we must be prepared for
fluctuation of creative power. Mr. Eliot has written of this:

[1] These are the manuscript headings for the B text of the poem as reproduced in Skeat's edition, *op. cit.*
[2] See the articles by Wells and Coghill referred to above, p. 5.
[3] A. H. Smith, *Piers Plowman and the Pursuit of Poetry* (London, 1950), p. 19.
[4] J. Lawlor, 'The Imaginative Unity of *Piers Plowman*', R.E.S., N.S. VIII (1957) p. 126.
[5] *Ibid.*, p. 124.   [6] *Ibid.*, p. 126.

... in a poem of any length, there must be transition between passages of greater
and less intensity to give a rhythm of fluctuating emotion necessary to the musical
structure of the whole: and the passages of less intensity will be, in relation to the
level on which the total poem operates, prosaic ... so that in the sense implied by
that context, *no poet can write a poem of amplitude unless he is a master of the prosaic*.[1]

The discipline of writing and reading any long poem is one which
asks for stamina on the part of the poet, an ability to manage the
'transitions' without disrupting the large flow of the poem, and,
on the part of the reader, a sympathetic willingness to move from
one level to another, an acceptance of heights and depressions as
they succeed one another. And this is true whether we are considering *Piers Plowman*, *The Prelude*, or *Paradise Lost*. None of these
poets can be condemned for his 'prosaic poetry'; in many ways
it is an essential condition of the total success of the work. Moreover, Langland is not, clearly, the sort of artist who

... before he has written his poem ... knows, and could state, the specifications
of it in the kind of way in which a joiner knows the specifications of a table
he is about to make ... what he wants to say is not present to him as an end
towards which means have to be devised; it becomes clear to him only as the
poem takes shape in his mind, or the clay in his fingers.[2]

These quotations usefully describe aspects of Langland's labour on
the poem as a whole, the one stressing ordered patterning, the other
spontaneous growth. Both order and spontaneity can be found in
Piers Plowman. But we must reaffirm that they occur in a specifically
religious context; the rhythm of the poem is strongly related to a
spiritual rhythm. What we have here is very similar to extempore
meditation or prayer upon set themes; the planned and the un-
planned alternate. The analogy with prayer leads us closer to the
conviction that this poem may not be a completely new literary
kind in his own period: that Langland had, perhaps, not one but
several models for the organization of his work. And his originality
may be proved to lie in the unique use he made of those models.

We have already seen that the typical Old and Middle English
alliterative poem, with its narrative constantly loaded and retarded
by description, comment and subsidiary episode of all kinds, is of
certain limited use as an introduction to *Piers Plowman*. Langland's
poem owes a measure of allegiance to this mode of composition, but
makes a *final* impression which differs from that of any major
alliterative work. If we turn away from alliterative verse to other
long religious poems Langland might have had in mind as models,

[1] *The Music of Poetry* (Glasgow, 1942), p. 18.
[2] R. G. Collingwood, *The Principles of Art* (Oxford, 1950), pp. 28-9.

we find the same partial and, therefore, unsatisfactory structural likenesses. The Miracle Play Cycles, taking as their scope man's history from Creation to the Last Judgement, bear some resemblance to Piers Plowman; a time span as comprehensive as this is a basic assumption of the poem, and on occasion the actual narrative sequence of the Passus runs parallel to that of the plays. In Passus XVII–XX of the B text, 'Crystes passioun and penaunce', the Resurrection, the establishment of an evangelical Church and the eventual attack of Antichrist are witnessed by the dreamer—revealing in Langland, it is interesting to note, a gift for dramatic situation and dialogue far beyond the capability of the average mediaeval religious play-writer. The differences, in fact, rather than the likenesses between *Piers Plowman* and the Miracle Plays are most significant. Langland's treatment of the Passion, Harrowing of Hell and Resurrection, vividly dramatic in places, is also far more learned; the range of allusion is wider, and the narrative is always liable to be halted by commentary of various sorts.[1] The fact that Langland chooses to stop his poem short of the final scene of the Miracle Plays—the Last Judgement—is an important proof of divergent aims.[2] Although the plays may have given Langland some help for individual passages, they could not, clearly, have provided him with a framework for the poem.

Nor could the other 'cyclical' compositions of the age—Biblical and Universal Histories such as the *Cursor Mundi*.[3] In those, certainly, Langland could have found precedent for a work which combined narrative—often dramatically set—with full didactic and legendary commentary on that narrative. But difficulties arise when more precise comparisons are made. The progress of *Piers Plowman* is so much more complicated and arbitrary than that of the sacred history, which lays out its varied material according to an easily recognizable scheme, and ties all comment to a main narrative. Here, perhaps, the crux of the matter is reached. All the works we have been considering are organized as narratives. Alliterative poem, miracle play or religious history, however much concerned with ideas, has an overall, even if interrupted, narrative plan. With *Piers Plowman* the case is different: it soon becomes apparent that

---

[1] The follow-up of the magnificently 'staged' episode in Hell, as Christ approaches (B.XVII.260–318) by Christ's long speech of justification to Satan (B.XVII.325–401) shows how much more complex are Langland's interests and intentions compared with those of the Miracle Play authors.

[2] See below, pp. 92 foll. and pp. 103–4.

[3] Ed. R. Morris (E.E.T.S., O.S. 57 etc.; 1874–93), 3 vols.

the unity and consistency of the poem cannot be most persuasively argued on narrative grounds. The story of the dreamer's adventures within his series of visions is *one* of the ways in which Langland's meaning is 'signposted' for us, but the full extent of that meaning will not be revealed if we are minutely preoccupied with the development of a narrative. It is the development of theme or themes which is of overriding importance, and which is served, not controlled, by means of a narrative. In this description, the general likeness between the poem and sermon literature comes once more to notice, encouraging us to inquire further and in greater detail.

The general plan of the poem as first outlined in earlier critical studies,[1] still seems to be acceptable. Starting from the manuscript headings, we can see how these four great divisions do, however roughly, correspond to well-defined stages in the poet's thought; whether we describe his major activity as the search for salvation, or for truth, as an investigation of the nature of the Trinity, of Divine Love, of the perfect life, it is still clear that the Prologue and Passus I–VII are introductory, laying down proposals for future development. Passus VIII–XV develop those proposals in discursive, circuitous 'inner' debate, Passus XVI–XVIII give us the fruit of that debate in visionary, illuminative terms, and Passus XIX–XX return the poem to its starting point, where the debate and the vision may begin to have widest operation in the individual and in his world. It is clear also that Piers Plowman is the main unifying link between the sections, symbolizing in his changing form many mediaeval institutions and ideas, and—more importantly—the poet's deepening comprehension of the vast Christian plan.

But our actual experience of the poem is rich, complex, and sometimes more confusing than the recognition of these formal divisions and links might lead us to expect. In addition to a narrative of tenuous continuity, there seem to be a score of themes under urgent consideration at any given moment: Langland is constantly distracted by fresh objects of interest: the four main sections merge imperceptibly and sometimes inexplicably, into one another, and the significance of Piers himself is open to question at many stages in the poem. When involved with the text our impression may often be that *Piers Plowman* is constructed

---

[1] Notably, those of Wells and Coghill. In the following discussion, reference is to the B version of the poem.

... d'après un plan dont la logique nous échappe, nourris d'associations, d'idées qui ne nous semblent ni naturelles ni surtout nécessaires.[1]

This comment on the procedures of mediaeval sermons bears strongly upon *Piers Plowman*. The elusive 'logic of the plan' of the poem can often be explained in the same terms as those appropriate to the literature of the mediaeval pulpit which, in its anxiety to produce the fullest possible 'drawing-out' of its stated themes, allowed, even encouraged, the modification of planned form by sudden departure from plan, and which maintained an over-all unity by a loose-knit, linking system of repetitions, correspondences and cross-references.[2]

Here the larger importance of the repetitive verbal devices discussed above becomes clearer. Exactly how powerful a force these (often widely-spaced) link-ups can exert towards the general unity of the poem is well illustrated by the episode of the Seven Deadly Sins in Passus V. This episode, which could perhaps be considered over-extensive if we are thinking in terms of a classically-proportioned unity, in fact, harks back imaginatively to Passus II, and the sinful retinue of Lady Meed, and forward to Passus XIII, with the description of the tattered cloak of Hawkin. Hawkin is the ordinary, sinful man before repentance; he is still 'encombred with sin', and so, allegorically, his cloak must be cleansed—it is

... bidropped with Wratthe.and wikked wille,
With Enuye and yuel speche.entysyng to fyʒte ...

                                        (B.XIII.321-2)

The vivid, pictorial detail of Passus V springs to mind—Wrath, 'nyvelynge with the nose. and his nekke hangynge', Envy who looked 'as a leke hadde yleye . longe in the sonne'. We remember also the detailed study of the nature and operation of such sins in that Passus. Hawkin's sinful cloak draws now upon a wide range of associations both pictorial and abstract which are realized briefly but powerfully in the verse of the following Passus XIV, as Patience enumerates the sins and their corrective—poverty (*ll.* 201 foll.). Again, in Passus XX, when the poem begins to come round full

---

[1] Gilson, *Les Idées et Les Lettres*, p. 95.
[2] Professor Coghill, in his British Academy Gollancz lecture, 'The Pardon of Piers Plowman', *Proc. Brit. Acad.*, XXX (1944), pointed out how the poem is full of echoes and foretastes, without relating this to sermon practice, but rather to 'the way his (Langland's) mind worked'. For a further consideration of repetition as a structural device in *Piers Plowman*, see E. Salter, 'Medieval Poetry and the Figural View of Reality', British Academy Gollancz lecture for 1968.

circle, with the attack of Antichrist, it seems natural that Pride bore
his banner, that Lechery 'leyde on . with a laughyng chiere', that
Sloth commanded 'proud prestes . moo than a thousand'. We are,
by now, thoroughly familiar with them; we have heard their
confessions, we have seen them in action. The truth expressed by
Hawkin himself, in Passus XIV, now comes home fully:

'Synne suweth us euere.' (*l.* 323)

The connections are not pointed for us explicitly by the poet;
he expects that we shall realize them, however, and that each
episode will be enriched by remembrance of what precedes it, even
if at some distance. Anticipations and echoes run the length of the
poem. A dramatic example occurs in Passus XVIII, at the very
climax of the work, the Harrowing of Hell. The passage has already
been commented upon for its internal verbal patterning; more
significant still is the way in which it calls up verbal and conceptual
reminiscences from far back in the poem, and twists diverse threads
into a firm knot.

'The biternesse that thow hast browe.brouke it thi-seluen,[1]
That art doctour of deth.drynke that thow madest!
For I, that am lorde of lyf.loue is my drynke,
And for that drynke to-day.I deyde vpon erthe.
I fauȝte so, me threstes ȝet.for mannes soule sake;
May no drynke me moiste.ne my thruste slake,
Tyl the vendage falle.in the vale of Iosephhath,
That I drynke riȝte ripe must.*resureccio mortuorum*,
And thanne shal I come as a kynge.crouned with angeles,
And han out of helle.alle mennes soules.'
(B.XVIII.362–370)

Almost every word in this passage has a deep resonance of sense
and sound.

Christ's name for Satan, 'doctour of deth', and the reference to
the bitter drink of his own making, links back not only to the
events of the Crucifixion, when the 'drink of death' was offered
to Christ:

. . . poysoun on a pole.thei put vp to his lippes,
And bede hym drynke his deth-yuel.his dayes were ydone.
(XVIII.52–3)[2]

and to the earlier recognition of Christ as 'leche of lyf' (XVI. 118),
but also catches up a far earlier episode—the Feast of Learned

[1] '. . . enjoy it yourself.'
[2] All references in this section are to the B text unless otherwise stated.

Doctors (XIII) to which the Dreamer and Patience were invited.
There, in the greedy eating and drinking of one learned professor

> 'Dowel?' quod this doctour—. and toke the cuppe and dranke—
>
> (XIII.103)

they witnessed hypocrisy and sterility; Satan's drink of sin and the
doctor's drink of pride are death, for they are a denial of love:

> 'Who so loueth nouʒte, leue me. he lyueth in deth-deyinge.'
>
> (XI.171)

The words also look forward to that other doctor, the friar Flattery
who, in Passus XX, is 'spiritual death' to Contrition, enchanting
him with his false physic, and thereby making necessary the final
pilgrimage to seek Piers Plowman. In the third line of the passage,
'lorde of lyf' is a phrase of wealthy associations. Christ's gift of
eternal life to man, by grace of God, is an idea which is stressed
more and more as the poem proceeds. In Passus IX.29, the Creator
is 'lorde of lyf and of lyghte'; in Passus XIII. 120 we hear of the castle

> 'There the lorde of Lyf wonyeth.'

Faith, dealing with the Trinity, speaks of the Holy Ghost as

> 'The liʒte of alle that lyf . . .'
>
> (XVI.189)

and Christ is referred to as giving 'lyf for lyf' (XVI.268). These
widely-scattered references are taken up and made into what could
almost be called a 'leit-motif' of Passus XVIII. Christ's struggle
is that of life and death:

> 'For a bitter bataille . . .
> Lyf and Deth in this derknesse. her one fordoth the other . . .'
>
> (XVIII.64–5)

When he died (XVIII.59)

> The lord of lyf and of liʒte. tho leyed his eyen togideres.

and Faith prophecies to the Jews that

> 'Lyf shal haue the maistrye . . .'
>
> (XVIII.102)

The 'lighte and leme' which approaches and bursts through into
Hell after the Resurrection is clearly the 'light of life' challenging
the 'darkness of death'.

'Loue is my drynke' picks up innumerable past references to the doctrine of love as a remedy for all the ills of man; from Passus I we have been hearing of it, increasingly connected with the name of Piers—Christ, who has

> '. . . sette alle sciences at a soppe.saue loue one.'
>
> (XIII.124)

In particular, we remember, from Passus XI, the introduction of the Christ's 'drink of love'—here prescribed for man by Christ himself:

> O *vos omnes scicientes, venite etc.*;
> And badde hem souke for synne.saufly at his breste,
> And drynke bote for bale.brouke it who so my3te.[1]
>
> (115–117)

The contest, which so increased Christ's thirst for souls—'I fau3te so, me threstes 3et . . .'—takes us back through all the battle imagery of this section of the poem (the jousting in Jerusalem, the armour of Piers Plowman, the 'bitter bataille' of life and death) to the lines in Passus I which describe the need of divine love to be further satisfied by assuming flesh and blood:

> 'For heuene my3te nou3te holden it.it was so heuy of hym-self,
> Tyl it hadde of the erthe.yeten his fylle—'
>
> (151–2)

In Passus XVIII Christ deepens this metaphor; the Incarnation did satisfy to some extent, but the final quenching of thirst (or hunger) will not be achieved until the gathering of human souls into Divine Love on Judgement Day. And here we merge the ideas of thirst and fruition in the embracing metaphor of the wine-harvest:

> 'May no drynke me moiste.ne my thruste slake,
> Tyl the vendage falle.in the vale of Iosephath—'

This calls up the preceding allegory of the Tree of Life, or Charity, upon which man grows as a ripening fruit,

> —Pieres fruit—
>
> (XVI.94)

to be picked, when ready, by Christ or the Devil:

> And thanne shulde Iesus Iuste therefore.bi Iuggement of armes,
> Whether shulde fonge the fruit.the fende or hymselue.[2]
>
> (XVI.95–6)

---

[1] '. . . and drink cure for evil—let all partake of it.' 'Brouke it who so my3te' links, in its turn, with the first line of the passage under consideration: 'brouke it thi-seluen'.

[2] '. . . whether the fiend or he himself should take the fruit.'

The ultimate contest, the ultimate draught of satisfaction, the ultimate harvest will be

'*resureccio mortuorum*'

Christ now pictured as the triumphant king 'crouned with angeles' completes and transposes into a different key all the teaching on kingship which occupied Langland so much in the early part of the poem. Christ, passing from knight jousting to king, fulfills, in a divine context, the ideal earthly pattern Langland had proposed:

Thanne come there a kyng.kny3thod hym ladde . . .

(Prol.112)

And it looks forward to another passage of 'resolution' in Passus XIX, where divine kingship is discussed, and we are taught by Conscience that 'knyghte, kynge, conqueroure . may be o persone' (27 foll.).

It would be foolish to assert that all these 'echoes' and 'fore-warnings' are deliberately arranged by Langland; their presence and effect is, however, undeniable. A passage such as this, in Passus XVIII, in its relationship to the rest of the poem, illustrates strikingly the quality of Langland's mind and art. He proposes main themes, leading ideas, which in statement, illustration and restatement are allowed to draw to themselves in great abundance and richness as many associations as will usefully serve to display their full meaning. The nature and function of sin, for instance, is a leading theme; this is announced early on, in Passus II when the dreamer begs Holy Church for some means of understanding what he has just seen in the dark Prologue:

'Kenne me bi somme crafte.to knowe the Fals . . .' (4)

It is pursued directly (in the Meed episodes and in the examination of the Seven Deadly Sins), is kept in mind in sections which have other major preoccupations (the sin of pride is bitterly castigated by Dame Studye in Passus X), is dealt with obliquely (in the Feast of learned Doctors, Passus XIII), is studied in a particular context (that of unreformed Active Life, Passus XIII), is set out as a religio-historical drama in Passus XVI–XVIII, and returns as an urgent contemporary question in Passus XIX. The nature and function of love in the universe is a leading theme—the main theme. And here again we perceive the same loose-linked method of procedure; Holy Church's words in Passus I

'Loue is leche of lyf. and nexte owre lorde selue,
And also the graith gate. that goth in-to heuene—'

(B.202–3)

are left, taken up and discussed, approached from various directions,
re-stated a score of times in the poem. The search to understand
the principle of all good lives, Dowel, Dobet, Dobest, leads back
in each case to the answer 'love'.[1] It is recommended as an essential
of life by Dame Studye,[2] is the subject of Trajan's speech against
rigid law in the following passus:[3]

Who so loueth nouȝte, leue me. he lyueth in deth-deyinge—'

is placed higher than learning by Clergye himself,[4] is defined in a
splendidly rhetorical, expansive speech by Anima[5] and becomes the
over-riding and triumphant subject of the central part of the poem,
the Crucifixion and Harrowing of Hell. Thus when Kynde counsels
the dreamer, near the end of the vision:

'Lerne to loue . . . and leue of alle othre.'

(B.XX.207)

we feel how the theme of love has spanned the poem, unifying it—
has been, in fact, like the theme of the loose mediaeval sermon,
developed in innumerable variations, each part being essential.[6]

In these cases, a loose-knit harmony of parts and whole can be
quite easily illustrated and experienced. And often a closer look
at what appear to be wilfully-developed episodes, discussions,
reveals the 'logique interne' to which Langland is working.

The great amount of space and time, for instance, which is given
up to the subject of Meed in the first part of the poem, may seem
to contribute little towards the general unity of the poem. The
allegory of the marriage, trial and condemnation of Lady Meed
takes up three Passus (B.II, III, IV) and is almost a separate entity.
Brilliant as it is, it does not link in a very obvious way with what is
to come. But, of course, it gives the poem a proper spiritual
direction; a detailed knowledge of the two kinds of Meed—true
and false reward—is most necessary if the characters in the allegory
and the observing dreamer are to be convinced that the meed which

[1] Definitions of all three as love are given in B.X.187, B.XII.30, B.IX.200, B.XIII.138.
[2] B.X. 206–7.   [3] B.XI.165 foll.   [4] B.XIII.124.   [5] B.XV.145 foll.
[6] It is interesting that Professor Donaldson, *op. cit.*, p. 143, note 6, while reasonably rejecting
Owst's view of the poem as 'the quintessence of English mediæval preaching', also rejects
the idea that there is anything in the sermons to explain 'the large plan of its great allegory'.

'... God of his grace. graunteth in his blisse
To tho that wel worchen. whil thei ben here.'
(B.III.231-2)

is the only one worth having. For they are to put their faith in a poor
plowman, who has nothing to offer them in return except faith
and love—ever-renewed effort, and the warmth of charity instead
of 'hot coles' on a winter's night. The lessons of patience, humility,
suffering, which pilgrims travelling with Piers must learn, can only
be welcomed by those who believe in God's meed:

'Heuene after her hennes-goynge ...'
(B.XIV.165)

and not that of man.

Similarly, the great care lavished on the establishment of Piers
as a vivid character in Passus V–VII may seem, at first, to be wasted,
considering how little we see of him in the rest of the poem and
how rarefied a creature he is in his later transformed appearances.
It might seem as if here is an example of Langland's uncertain
touch—an enthusiasm which did not last, a spontaneous and un-
directed piece of work. But those very purposes in the later part
of the allegory which demand the changed and seldom-seen Piers,
demand also the familiar figure of the early Passus. We must be
thoroughly at home with the honest plowman Piers, quick to anger
in the face of hypocrisy and laziness:

'Now, bi the peril of my soule!' quod Pieres. al in pure tene,
'But ȝe arise the rather. and rape ȝow to worche,[1]
Shal no greyne that groweth. glade ȝow at nede;
And tho ȝe deye for dole. the deuel haue that reccheth!'
(B.VI.119-22)

but full of compassion for his fellow men:

'They are my blody bretheren', quod Pieres. 'for god bouȝte vs alle;
Treuthe tauȝte me ones. to louye hem vchone—'
(B.VI.210-11)

And successive transformations undergone by Piers over the poem
must not cancel out our early impressions of his sturdy truth and
practical charity; however profound the spiritual matters he comes
to represent—'Petrus, id est Christus'—we must still be drawn
to him instinctively as to the plain-speaking man who had only

---

[1] ... and stir yourselves to work ...'

'. . . a cow and a kalf. and a cart-mare
To drawe a-felde my donge. the while the drought lasteth.'
(B.VI.289–90)

This is part of a design; Piers is firmly set in our respect and affection before he begins his arduous pilgrimage of change. In his long absences and in his later altered appearances the plowman is always remembered. Hence the resolve 'to seke Piers the Plowman' in the last lines of the poem is as Langland meant it to be, an urgent move towards a real, living creature, as well as a restatement of an ideal.

But if we are tempted, by such material, to hold unconditionally that this is a poem of plan and purpose, building irresistibly by means of links, echoes, and expansions structurally desirable towards a vast total unity, then we should recollect one important precept of the preaching manuals:

. . . Edification of souls is more to be prized than continuity of discourse.[1]

In Langland's poem this law operates too. Just as the preacher was licensed to improvise, to change direction or metaphor upon impulse—or rather, upon conviction that such action was in the best interests of the spiritual well-being of his audience—so Langland clearly assumes that unity is subservient to moral fruitfulness. We can see in *Piers Plowman*, sometimes, the 'déplacements brusques des prédicateurs', the movement away from announced themes 'chaque fois que son zèle pour les âmes propose à son imagination quelque nouvel objet'.[2] On two occasions, at least, Langland acknowledges that he has been diverted from his theme;[3] there are many other similar occasions when no explicit comment is made. The long speech by Witte (B.IX.1–206) on the subject of Dowel, Dobet and Dobest, is an example. Beginning in answer to the dreamer's desire to know 'where Dowel, Dobet and Dobest ben in londe', Witte proposes the allegory of Sir Dowel's Castle. In this castle, which, with its lady, Anima, is 'man with a soule', Dowel, Dobet and Dobest live at peace: the creator of the castle is Kynde. So far, all is systematic. But at *l.* 25 the dreamer interrupts to ask 'What kynnes thyng is Kynde'. This in itself looks like a dramatic rendering of the preacher's sudden decision to make one important point clearer for his audience; at any rate, both the allegory and the theme of Dowel are halted, while Witte celebrates Kynde—the 'gret god that gynnynge had neuere'—and the creation

---

[1] Gilson, *op. cit.*, p. 143.   [2] *Ibid.*, p. 144.   [3] B.XI.309, C.XXI.360–2.

of man. Returning to the allegory, he devotes himself to the guard of the castle, Inwit, who stands, it seems, for the God-directed intellect of man, the rational power of the soul. After this, the allegory is dropped: the poet's attention is taken up by Inwit and those classes of people who misuse or lack it. By now we have moved from exposition to denunciation and exhortation. Gluttons, whose 'god is her wombe', are castigated: the Church is rebuked for neglecting those who have not the 'inwit' to help themselves. Although Langland tries to curb himself here:

> Of this matere I myȝte.make a longe tale . . . (*l.* 71)

he is led on, irresistibly, to other examples of injustice towards the helpless: unkind godparents, worldly prelates. He also manages to include a side-blow at Christians in general for not being as charitable as Jews towards their fellow men. The theme of Dowel is then explicitly resumed for a while, but with the mention of 'trewe wedded libbing folk' (*l.* 107), the poet feels it necessary to inform about the good and evil progeny of Eve, and to give a brief résumé of the Flood before making a wholesale attack upon contemporary loveless, 'business' marriages. The speech then draws itself up (*ll.* 199 foll.) with a compact definition of Dowel, Dobet and Dobest which comes at this stage as somewhat of a surprise. Although the whole passage does, in a very loose sense, deal with the 'three good lives', it does not develop smoothly according to any definable plan, but rather according to the poet's 'zèle pour les âmes'. He allows himself to enlarge upon any aspect of the subject which seems rewarding: the creation of man, the hypocrisy of the Church, mediaeval marriage-broking, Jew against Christian.

Similarly, in the long speech by Ymagynatyf (B.XII.30 foll.) we begin with a statement about love and obedience; in the midst of examples of those whose misfortune was due to disobedience (Lucifer, Job) we pass to those whose sin was the over-prizing of material things—Alexander, fair Rosamund. Here Langland cannot, apparently, resist a short diatribe against the rich; their possessions are death to the soul. The discussion has already shown a liking for the tangential. We now begin on what looks like another main theme: the ground of grace, from which Clergye and Kynde Witte spring. The importance of the interaction of both is stressed; the dreamer is taught that knowledge can be of immense help in salvation of souls, and rebuked for having assumed glibly that unlearned men have a better chance of heaven than learned.

With a slightly surprising transition, we then turn to consider those things beyond the understanding of Clergye and Kynde Witte; some things, says Ymagynatyf, are only known by Nature (Kynde). This calls out a very moving passage of poetry (*ll.* 227 foll.) about the instinctive knowledge imparted to birds, beasts and man by Nature, in which the peacock is mentioned. Here it seems that some chord in Langland's learned memory was touched; the peacock is a useful similitude for the rich, who are uselessly encumbered by possessions, and cry in vain to Christ on their death day. This bestiary exemplum is followed up by that of the lark, which is likened to 'lowe-lybbing' men in its swift flight to heaven. Acknowledging the ultimate sources of such religious natural history in Aristotle, 'the grete clerke', Ymagynatyf returns to the theme of learning and salvation, decides that we cannot tell whether such learned pagan doctors are saved, and finishes with a devout committal of the matter to the grace of God. It can be seen that while nothing here is entirely disconnected from its surrounding matter, the flow of thought does take some fairly sharp turns and checks. Twice Ymagynatyf pauses in the development of the speech—which is mainly concerned with learning and salvation—to warn against the evil of riches. We proceed by a very loose association of ideas: 'magis . . . aedificatio quam . . . continuatio'.

With these reservations, we can see the larger unity of *Piers Plowman* in two ways. First, there is the structure of which the manuscripts tell us: four sections occupied with searches along narrative and reflective paths for the states of Dowel, Dobet and Dobest. These sections are linked by the presence of the dreamer, and by the appearances of and references to Piers Plowman. There is a cyclic plan to the whole; the poem ends where it began. Secondly, there is a continuous process of linking and cross-referencing of sound and idea; themes and sub-themes are treated often on musical lines, weaving and echoing in many different variations. Thus however disjointed or even confusing the actual narrative may become, the themes of the poem are building up to large conclusions. We may not be quite sure of allegorical locations, the coming and going of characters, even the exact division of speeches between them, but we *are* sure of our gradual, though indirect, movement towards truth by way of love.

E

(iii) *The Vision*

But there is a third kind of unity in *Piers Plowman* which, however little we may be critically aware of it, helps us to accept both the frequent dislocation of the general plan of the poem, and the suspension, the delay of link-ups in sense and sound. If, as seems certain, Langland was deeply and continuously indebted to mediaeval sermon technique for ways of organizing his poem, by enclosing that whole poem within a dream he made it so much more than what one writer has called it—'the quintessence of English mediaeval preaching'.[1]

Not that the act of setting *Piers Plowman* as a dream need in itself have been specially significant. It is true that the Middle Ages showed considerable interest in the nature and meaning of dreams— an interest which was fed by the works of the Church Fathers, and by Biblical and Classical literature.[2] Following upon the adoption of the dream-form for the great French thirteenth-century allegory, the *Roman de la Rose*, countless European poets prefaced secular and religious material with a dream-introduction.[3] No doubt, apart from gaining literary prestige by using a 'convention' already so established and famous, many authors felt that presentation as a dream added force and authority to what they had to say: if scientific opinion held that some dreams were valueless, it also taught that others

> . . . signifiaunce be
> Of good and harm to many wightes.[4]

But the larger 'signifiaunce' of dreams is not always in the mediaeval poet's mind. The dream is often summarily used; a brief reference to sleep contents the author, and the rest of the work proceeds independently. It is often ornamental—the window which opens upon a specially selected, idealized landscape; there the dreamer may witness the acting-out of fantasy or realism, a love-story or a moral debate. The removal of dreamer and reader from

[1] Owst, *Preaching in Mediaeval England*, p. 295.

[2] The most important source of information (on which Chaucer, for instance, drew heavily) was the fifth century Commentary by Macrobius upon the *Somnium Scipionis* (originally part of the sixth book of Cicero's *De Re Publica*). Here mediaeval authors found 'scientific' classifications of various kinds of dream, according to their origins and influences. See *Macrobius's Commentary on the Dream of Scipio*, tr. W. H. Stahl (New York, 1952).

[3] See D. L. Owen, *Piers Plowman. A Comparison with some Earlier and Contemporary French Allegories* (London, 1912), Chapter III.

[4] *Romaunt of the Rose, ll.* 16–17 (Chaucerian translation), ed. Robinson, *op. cit.*, p. 664. Chaucer's *Parliament of Fouls*, which is 'dreamed' after a reading of Macrobius, uses the dream with point as well as grace. See J. A. W. Bennett, *The Parlement of Foules* (Oxford, 1957), pp. 51 foll.

the associations of the waking world is utilized, in the main, as a literary convenience: it allows the poet scope for display of descriptive and dramatic abilities, for undisturbed analysis of sentiment, or indulgence of fancy. The dream in *Piers Plowman* has a different function.

In few other mediaeval poems are we so directly impressed with the personal and universal importance of the dream-experience: there is a sense of increasing urgency about the whole process of sleeping and waking which contrasts strongly with the normal run of dream-poems. Thus, although Chaucer makes frequent use of the dream-form in his earlier poems (the *Book of the Duchess*, the *House of Fame*, the *Parliament of Foules*) and discusses dreams with such freedom and intelligence, his work is quite different in atmosphere and direction from *Piers Plowman*. Typically unwilling to commit himself to a judicial statement on the value of what he dreams, he is more concerned with rationalizing a dream than with proving its oracular nature. Only one work of Langland's day is to any degree comparable with Piers Plowman—the anonymous *Pearl*.[1] In both poems the movement into the dream is conceived as the passage from the semblance of reality into reality itself—a journey only made possible by the grace of God. This is clarified by the *Pearl* poet very early on:

Fro spot my spyryt þer sprang in space;
My body on balke þer bod in sweuen.[2]
My goste is gone in Godeȝ grace
In auenture ther mervayleȝ meuen.

(*ll.* 61–4)

And the further the dreamer of *Piers Plowman* progresses into the substance of his dreams, the clearer it becomes that this also is an 'auenture' reached only 'in Godes grace'. The specifically religious context of sleep becomes more marked. So, after the first awakening, the dreamer, already longing to go deeper into the world of his dreams, falls swiftly asleep as he says his prayers:

And so I babeled on my bedes.thei brouȝte me a-slepe.
(B.V.8)

If it is prayer which induces sleep, it is not strange to find the dreamer reflecting, in the next waking interlude (B.VII.139 foll.), upon the nature of dreams, and asserting the seriousness of what he has been

[1] See above, p. 18, n. 1. Ed. E. V. Gordon (Oxford, 1952).
[2] '. . . my body remained in sleep upon the mound . . .'

allowed to see by examples taken from the Bible. The dreams of Daniel and Joseph

> maketh me. on this meteles[1] to thynke;
>
> (B.VII.167)

The revelatory, prophetic value of the dream is henceforward not to be forgotten. Lessons of particular significance are conveyed by a dream within a dream; the unfortunate dreamer, brought suddenly back from this deeper world because of his unauthorized questioning, is reminded of what he has forgone:

> '. . . for thine entermetyng. here artow forsake . . .
> Adam, while he spak nou3t. had paradys at wille . . .'[2]
>
> (B.XL.406, 407)

When he sleeps again, he acknowledges openly that his dreams are in the will of Christ:

> And, as Cryste wolde, there come Conscience. to conforte me that tyme . . .
>
> (B.XIII.22)

As we come nearer to the heart of the poem, with the great theme of Charity focused in the person of Piers the Plowman, the intervals between dream and dream are suffered with growing impatience. Awake, nothing is real; the dreamer's perception has been heightened, and the proud folly of the contemporary world maddens him—

> Tyl Resoun hadde reuthe on me. and rokked me aslepe . . .
>
> (B.XV.11)

The next 'dream within a dream' brings the long-awaited entry of Piers and prepares the dreamer for his sight of the Passion and Resurrection. Naturally, he comes from sleep with reluctance, and the line

> Tyl I wex wery of the worlde. and wylned eft to slepe . . .
>
> (B.XVIII.4)

which prefaces his vision of 'Crystes passioun and penaunce', is, in its context, no escapist wish, but an eager desire to return to the source of life. Waking from this vision, his first impulse is to worship before the Cross, and then to write down what he has seen. Almost immediately

---

[1] '. . . dream . . .'

[2] So too, in *Pearl*, the dreamer is cast out of sleep because of a momentary failure of faith and obedience: his dream is a revelation of divine grace which, had he not erred, might have proceeded 'to more of his mysteries'.

In myddes of the masse.tho men ʒede to offrynge,[1]
I fel eftsones a-slepe . . .

(B.XIX.4-5)

The last stages of his dream-experience are underway—he witnesses
the Resurrection, and the establishment of the Christian Church.
Thus the last words of the poem—'til I gan awake'—do not simply
mark a formal artistic conclusion: they mark the end of a vision of
ultimate truth.

In many mediaeval dream poems, sleep represents a state of
privilege to which the dreamer would not normally, in waking life,
attain. In *Piers Plowman* it has added force: it represents a state of
grace. This is not, in quality or function, the sleep which brought
Guillaume de Lorris and poets like him into paradisaical gardens of
love. It is much more akin to the spiritual 'sleep' into which the
contemplative is admitted so that he may receive illumination:
'Ego dormio, et cor meum vigilat'.[2] The Middle Ages often
used this text as a metaphor of spiritual activity: St. Bernard
describes how

. . . ipsa quidem dormit, sed cor ejus vigilat, quo utique interim veritatis arcana
rimatur: quorum postmodum memoria statim ad se reditura pascatur.[3]

And the Englishman, Walter Hilton, commenting in Langland's
day upon the same spiritual processes, provides us with a passage
which has more relevance than any other 'dream-literature' of the
period to this sleep which can capture the poet's senses as he prays
or kneels at mass:

. . . *Ego dormio, et cor meum vigilat.* I sleep and my heart waketh. . . . The more
I sleep from outward things, the more wakeful am I in knowing of Jhesu and of
inward things. I may not wake to Jhesu, but if I sleep to the world . . . The more
that the eyes are shut in this manner sleep from the appetite of earthly thing, the
sharper is the inner sight in lovely beholding of heavenly fairhead. This sleeping
and this waking love worketh through the light of grace in the soul of the lover
of Jhesu.[4]

Needless to say, the revelations made to Langland's dreamer
as he 'sleeps to the world' are not identical with those high intimations

---

[1] '. . . when men went up to the offering . . .'
[2] *Canticles*, V.2. See also *Job* 33. 15 foll.: 'In a dream, in a vision of the night, when deep
sleep falleth upon men, . . . then he openeth the ears of men . . .'.
[3] *De Gradibus Humilitatis* ed. G. B. Burch (Harvard University Press, 1942), p. 164.
   '(it) sleeps itself, but its heart waketh, with which it searches out the secrets of truth, that
   it may feed on the memory of them when it returns to itself.'
For comment on the significance of 'sleep' in St. Bernard's works, see E. Gilson, *The Mystical
Theology of St. Bernard* (London, 1940), pp. 104-5.
[4] *The Scale of Perfection*, ed. E. Underhill (London, 1923), Book II, Chapter 40.

of 'heavenly fairhead' made to the mystic. The dreamer in *Piers Plowman* learns many things in sleep, ranging the whole area of the spiritual life; much of what he has to be taught has long been understood by those for whom St. Bernard and Hilton write. But he does come through the dream to comprehend, if not experience, a great mystery, and the dream unifies the whole poem in a specially powerful way. The strangeness of the happenings, even those very dislocations and delays which some critics would have us believe hinder our understanding, are made acceptable not simply in terms of the irrationality of the dreaming self and of the dream world, but in terms of the divine order of naturalness which prevails when once we are 'laid asleep in body, and become a living soul'. By this, Langland raises his poem on to a high level of originality. The dreamer is moved, without fully understanding reasons or route, from one place or discussion to another; his will, at first hesitant, resistant, is gradually made subject to a higher power, as the visionary's will is subject to God's. And through the dreamer, the reader is involved: the strange and compelling need to endure whatever is to come works strongly throughout the poem, affecting both. Thus, however tangential the poem's course may become, no material can ever seem entirely irrelevant. We can pass from dramatic exchange to deep revelation, from moral discourse to reflection without having to demand 'why': we know ourselves to be 'in auenture ther mervayles meuen'. In company with the dreamer, we come to accept the unheralded arrivals and departures of the chief character of the poem, Piers Plowman himself, as visitations of greatest import, sent by grace to aid the perplexed spirit of man on its journey through chaos and illumination towards 'St. Truth'. Like mystic and dreamer, we learn, as we sleep and wake, not to question what 'love worketh through the light of grace in the soul of the lover of Jhesu'.

Langland is a poet who does not deal in compromises. The conditions which are necessary for his most brilliant writing account for his most prosaic. He works to his greatness not by private experiment and exercise, but by wrestling, before us, with the challenge his enterprise throws out to him. For him it is artistically and spiritually proper that the triumphant, positive events of the Crucifixion and Harrowing of Hell (Passus XVI–XVIII) should be preceded by the tentative wanderings of Passus VII–XV. So, too, with the allegory and verse technique. Lady Meed, Hawkin, Gluttony, Wrath, and, above all, Piers, created by an imagination working powerfully and subtly, have as inevitable companions, the thin 'do-as-you-would-be-done-by' personifications: they are the raw material for growth. By refusing his allegory any special artistic privileges, Langland ensures that its range will be extreme— from the most dull to the most vital. Similarly, if he had not allowed into his verse all the multifarious crudities and irregularities of the spoken language, if he had not risked at every turn, becoming banal, garrulous, obscene, he would probably never have written, with a simplicity and economy that almost defies analysis:

> Ac Marie Magdaleyne. mette hym bi the wey,
> Goynge toward Galile. in godhed and manhed,
> And lyues and lokynge. and she aloude cryde,
> In eche a compaignye there she cam.
>   'Christus resurgens'!
>   (B.XIX.152–5)

And if he had not served us, pedantically, at times, with what he knew of the language of learning:

> And he brou3te vs of *Beati-quorum*. of *Beatus-virres* makynge,
> *Et-quorum-tecta-sunt-. peccata* in a disshe . . .
>   (B.XIII.53–4)

we should have missed the sonorous macaronic lines in which the climax of the Christian drama is reached:

> 'What lorde artow?' quod Lucifer. '*quis est iste*'?
> '*Rex glorie*'. the li3te sone seide,
> 'And lorde of my3te and of mayne. and al manere vertues; *dominus virtutum*;' . . .
> Patriarkes and prophetes. *populus in tenebris*
> Songen seynt Iohanes songe. '*ecce agnus dei*'
>   (B.XVIII. 314–16, 321–2)

The 'spiritual preoccupation', which affects *some* of his poetry adversely, is exactly what guarantees that his finest composition will be of a rare and special kind, springing directly out of something we can only call inspiration:

. . . a sodeyn steryng, & as it were vnauisid, speedly springing unto God as sparcle fro the cole . . .[1]

It is not inappropriate to use words from a mystical text to describe the working of Langland's greatest verse; more than any other mediaeval poet he feels himself to be committed to the rarest of all purposes, and like the mystics, his art is inseparable from his vision.

---

[1] ' . . . a sudden stirring, unexpected, as it were, springing swiftly to God like a spark from a live coal.' *The Cloud of Unknowing*, ed. P. Hodgson (E.T.S·E., O.S. 218, 1958), p. 22.

Poetic energy is generated in him by spiritual forces; he is most movingly articulate on themes such as suffering and love which not only attract to themselves all of his human pity and imagination, but reveal his ultimate dedication to God. So, in the midst of a passage of competent, unremarkable writing, the mere mention of the Incarnation brings a sudden and unexpected stirring, and the poetry responds:

> For the heihe holigoste.heuene shal to-cleue,
> And loue shal lepe out after.in-to this lowe erthe,
> And clennesse shal cacchen it . . .
>
> (B.XII.142–4)

Sensitivity to words and rhythms, an eye for the dramatic, the grotesque, a feeling for the pathetic, go to make Langland an *interesting* poet—but when he is a *great* poet, it is by reason of

> . . . þe drawȝt of this loue, and þe voise of þis cleping.[1]
>
> (*The Cloud*, p. 14)

---

[1] 'the drawing of this love and the voice of this calling,' trans. T. S. Eliot, *Little Gidding*.

CHAPTER III

THE ALLEGORY OF *PIERS PLOWMAN*: NATURE AND MEANING

(i) *The Nature of the Allegory*

When Langland falls asleep, he not only takes us into his dream, but shows us a landscape which is more than it might appear at first to be: the tower, the plain, the deep dale invite interpretation. They are, as is made clear by the dreamer, and later, by Holy Church, spiritual points of reference as well as imaginable realities, the dramatic backcloth to the events of the whole poem:

'What this montaigne bymeneth.and the merke dale,
And the felde ful of folke.I shal ȝow faire schewe.'

(B.I.1–2))

Here we embark upon a process of inquiry into significance which continues at varying tempo until the dark battle scenes of the concluding Passus. Langland's visions are given a predominantly allegorical mode of expression, and if we are to come at the fullness of his meaning, we have to decide how allegory functions in the poem.[1]

In a recent book on *Piers Plowman* which sets out to 'describe its form and explain its meaning',[2] the author states that he will read the poem 'as a literal rather than an allegorical poem', and will be looking for 'literal rather than hidden, second, or higher meanings'.[3] At the other extreme, another fairly recent study[4] assumes that Langland's meaning is almost always susceptible of analysis according to the fourfold method of interpretation commonly applied to the Biblical text in the Middle Ages. According to this view, literal, allegorical, tropological and anagogical meanings abound, and it is our task, like that of the eighth-century scholar of Turin to 'see beneath the letter's veil'[5] to the deepest hidden truth. Most critics have been convinced, to a greater or lesser degree, of the presence of multiple senses in the poem, and

[1] The following remarks upon Langland's allegory are supplemented by E. Salter and D. Pearsall, *Piers Plowman* (York Medieval Texts, 1967), pp. 9–28.
[2] R. W. Frank, *op. cit.*, p. ix.   [3] *Ibid.*, p. 2.
[4] D. W. Robertson and B. F. Huppé, *op. cit.*
[5] Quoted by B. Smalley, *The Study of the Bible in the Middle Ages* (Oxford, 1952), p. 1.

65

the general supposition has been that, even if the four senses are not consistently present, they are to be reckoned with at various stages in the text. As for the quality of Langland's allegorical creations, judgements have ranged from enthusiastic admiration to faint praise.

The newcomer to *Piers Plowman*, faced with such conflicting opinions, might reasonably deduce only that the poem upon which they are based is of a varied allegorical nature. In this chapter it will be proposed that Langland's allegory, seen in its particular mediaeval context, is certainly often many-stranded; sometimes its significance can be usefully, though not exclusively, defined according to the four-fold exegetical method. It proceeds by a succession of different allegorical modes, working changeably, sometimes rapidly, with local and global applications. While themes are being built up broadly and consistently, the allegory itself at times dispenses with strict continuity in every detail—the precept 'magis . . . aedificatio quam . . . continuatio'[1] has an importance here too. For these practices Langland can find partial sanction in many other mediaeval texts, both prose and verse, learned and popular, but his own resolution is unique.

Perhaps the first matter to be reaffirmed (since so much recent criticism has been engaged upon denying the symbolic content of mediaeval literature) is the familiarity of the whole mediaeval period, early and late, with art in which meaning overlaid meaning, or, by a more accurate metaphor, in which there are concentric circles of meaning, radiating from a given point. It is, of course, in the religious field that the richest evidence of multiple consciousness is found. And this is natural; Christianity built on a Judaic theory of history which believed that past and future were part of a planned design. The moral purpose of this design could be deduced from a study of phenomena and events.[2] As Christianity reshaped and developed this philosophy, the Old Testament was regarded more and more as a spiritual foreshadowing of the New; the historical facts were never disregarded, but tremendous stress was laid on the mystical correspondences which could be discovered from a comparison of Old and New. As early as the second century the four leading 'senses' of the whole Bible were formulated— literal, Christo-centric, moral and mystical—and rapidly became

---

[1] See above, Chapter II, pp. 55 foll.
[2] See Auerbach, *op. cit.*, Chapters I and II in particular, for comment upon the 'multi-layeredness' of Jewish literature which formed the basis of the Christian tradition.

the directive principle of Biblical exegesis.[1] And although the importance of the literal sense was increasingly stated from the twelfth and thirteenth centuries onwards, the mediaeval Christian did not lose, at any time, the apprehension of the temporal, the particular, as one aspect only of an eternal truth. The coexistence, the harmony of literal and spiritual significances is a basic mediaeval assumption, whether these significances are expressed precisely in the fourfold classification of Biblical scholarship or not.[2] These words (translated imaginatively from Hugh of St. Victor[3]) describe the 'divine harmony' of the Biblical text, but they could be used to describe the general mediaeval outlook upon the relationship between the natural and the supernatural world—a relationship established by God:

... la suavité de son sens spirituel qui nous émeut comme le jeu des cordes, ... la belle solidité de son sens littéral, qui, plein de mystères, s'étend sous les cordes comme une caisse de résonance, permettant de les tendre, de les accorder les unes aux autres, de faire résonner plus agréablement encore leur voix sonore.

No better working example of this could be found for mediaeval man, learned or simple, than the life of Christ. Here the historical facts were recommended to him in all their 'belle solidité' of warmth and poignancy, but the greater spiritual resonance of every spoken word and felt experience could never be forgotten. The Lives of Christ, Latin and vernacular, which provided both information and suitable commentary upon that information, stress equally the physical realities—the Birth, Passion and Death—and the high cosmic drama which such realities 'signify'. Thus while Christ suffered in Gethsemane, and the disciples slept, a great and agonizing debate proceeded in Heaven between God and the Heavenly Host on the necessity of the sacrifice of Christ; while Christ suffered the literal course of the Crucifixion, the Divine Being contemplated the working out of his intent, and the gates of Hell began to tremble.[4] Poets, prose writers, painters and sculptors saw to it that mediaeval man realized, even if in a very simple way, how events and objects

[1] See B. Smalley, *op. cit.*, for a complete account of Biblical interpretation in the Middle Ages.
[2] It is interesting that as late as the fifteenth century treatises on multiple interpretation were still being copied in England: see R. H. Bowers, 'A Middle English Treatise on Hermeneutics', *P.M.L.A.*, LXV (1950).
[3] By E. de Bruyne, *op. cit.*, II. 343, in his important Chapter VII, 'La Théorie de l'Allégorisme.'
[4] This 'doubleness' of action can be seen in most effective form in the relevant chapters of Nicholas Love's *Mirror of the Blessed Life of Christ* (see above, p. 26), a text of the later Middle Ages with great influence among all classes of readers.

existed in a wide and deep spiritual context,[1] and how vision and understanding of these phenomena might change, fluctuate mysteriously. This feeling for the potential 'resonance' of the literal, material, historical, is clearly expressed in literature as popularly directed as the mediaeval English lyrics which see *through* the Nativity, the child of the Virgin, to all the pain and shame of the Passion; his weeping and laughter mean, by powerful extension, the Fall and the Redemption of man:

> She sayde, 'dere sone, ly styll and slepe.
> What cause hast thu so sore to wepe . . .'
> 'Moder,' he sayde, 'for mane I wepe so sore
> And for hys loue I shall be tore . . .'[2]

In pictorial terms, there are the Crucifixion scenes, where the Cross and the dead Christ are backed by a sky filled with the agitated beating of angelic wings, and a pensive God gazes down.[3] There are the ivory carvings which may take as subject one particular moment in the celebration of the Mass, but draw in the whole mystery and aspiration of that moment by a deliberately formalized representation—a half-realistic, half-ideal plastic space which accommodates priest, singing deacons and angels perfectly.[4] This unaffected concern with 'a mystical reality . . . here present . . .'[5] is what informs the best art of the Middle Ages; the perception of the immediate object or scene is often the sharper because of the long perspectives behind them.

It is important to stress these things because the dramatic choice between a literal and a symbolic approach to a poem or picture— a choice which some recent critics would have us make—is an unnatural requirement for most mediaeval works of art, especially for those which take allegorical form. Whether Langland, or any other poet of his time, not writing for an exclusively learned audience, and using allegory, it should be stressed, for *elucidation* of spiritual matters, would have agreed that at its highest peaks his poem had four levels of meaning, to be described by the

---

[1] Auerbach, *op. cit.*, p. 43, puts this dramatically:
'the antagonism between sensory appearance and meaning . . . which permeates the early, and indeed the whole, Christian view of reality.'
[2] *Religious Lyrics of the Fifteenth Century*, ed. Carleton Brown (Oxford, 1939), p. 8.
[3] The Deposition, for instance, from the *Grandes Heures de Rohan* (XVth century) ed. J. Porcher (Skira, 1943).
[4] See R. Hinks, *Carolingian Art* (London, 1935), pp. 158–9, and Plate XVI.
[5] *Ibid.*, p. 159.

familiar exegetical system, is very uncertain.[1] It is certain, however, that he would have expected us to be receptive to various sorts of significances, and not necessarily to only one at a time. The proper test is not, ultimately, the historical probability of multiple meaning, but what we find irresistible in our experience of the work.

A comparison of the central section of *Piers Plowman* (B. Passus XVI-XVIII) with formally written allegories of the fourteenth century such as *The Desert of Religion*[2] or *The Abbey of the Holy Ghost*[3] confirms the impression that Langland's art is rich, of many-stranded significance. However Langland himself would have defined the differences, it is undeniable that, in these Passus, four senses of the Passion of Christ are constantly in mind—in the mind of the reader, and (it does not seem unreasonable to deduce) in the mind of the poet too. The literal meaning—the physical, agonizing event—is powerfully present. Then the allegorical— the meaning viewed in terms of the relationship between Christ and man; here the Passion signifies Christ's sacrifice for man, the gift of a way to salvation through Death, Resurrection and Harrowing of Hell. In its tropological or purely moral sense, the Crucifixion teaches that each human life must be centred about love and self-lessness: 'Fiat voluntas tua'. The anagogical truth of the matter turns on mystical surrender to God in perfect love—the dying of self in an ecstasy of communion with God. All such meanings, distinct yet connected, are present at this stage of the poem: the hinterland to Calvary is the allegorical debate among the four daughters of God about man's destiny and Christ's sacrifice:[4] the dreamer, witnessing divine love suffering, learns his 'moral' lesson of love, and the coalescing of the figures of Piers, the Good Samaritan, and Charity into the final triumphant figure of Christ,

---

[1] Dante's statements in the *Convivio*, Tractate II, section I (trans. W. W. Jackson, Oxford, 1909) beginning 'Writings can be understood and ought to be expounded chiefly in four senses' (p. 73 foll.) need not, of course, refer to his own practice in composition of poetry.

De Bruyne, *op. cit.*, II. 330, points to the dangers of thinking too categorically in terms of 'fourfold meaning' even in religious contexts. What we know of Biblical exegesis must not lead to interpret '*toute* la poésie médiévale en fonction de l'allégorisme'. Nevertheless, he is convinced of an inevitable movement towards richly allegorical thinking and writing in the Middle Ages:

'lorsque les poètes . . . s'inspirent de l'Écriture et même simplement de la Nature, *puisque dans la structure des faits historiques et physiques Dieu a inscrit la figure de réalités surnaturelles et mystérieuses, ne faut-il pas supposer que dans toutes les œuvres, il y a moins un germe de significa-tion allégorique . . .*', II. 333-4.

See the important discussion of multiple interpretation in pp. 1-82 of *Critical Approaches to Mediæval Literature*, ed. D. Bethurum (Columbia University Press, 1960).

[2] Ed. W. Hübner, *Archiv.* CXXVI (1911), pp. 58 foll.

[3] Ed. C. Horstman, *Yorkshire Writers. Richard Rolle of Hampole* (London, 1895), I.321 foll.   [4] B.XVIII.112 foll.

is most naturally understood in mystical terms of reference. At
times, when the poetry is full and persuasive, all these aspects of a
unifying truth gain simultaneous expression:

> 'For I, that am lorde of lyf.loue is my drynke,
> And for that drink to-day.I deyde vpon erthe.'
>
> (B.XVIII.362–3)

It is unnecessary to demand that Langland should demonstrate
to his audience the types and numbers of meaning he is calling up
at any given moment; he is not, after all, writing sermon, exegetical
or mystical treatise, but a poem which avails itself of many of their
techniques, topics and modes of thought in the service of one great
devotional and imaginative project—the quest for the 'treasure
of truth' by way of love. If Langland did not see this quest as an
investigation on four clearly distinguished levels of reality, he
certainly did see it as a journey into fullest implications. Any
attempt to limit his meaning—except where the text makes it
absolutely clear that this is required—is mistaken.

For there are times, it must be admitted, when he deliberately
confines himself to working in a particular mode which has no
easily discernible symbolic relevance, or which, perhaps, has a
stronger local than total symbolic relevance. He can pass from the
meaningful, 'layered' lines

> 'And that knoweth no clerke.ne creature in erthe,
> But Piers the Plowman. *Petrus, id est, Christus.*'
>
> (B.XV.205–6)

to lines such as this—

> '3e, bawe!' quod a brewere.'I wil nou3t be reuled'
>
> (B.XIX.394)

which are not manipulated powerfully, but have an immediate,
limited dramatic significance. Even, however, at its most obviously
literal, his poetry contributes to an overall allegorical meaning
which can be usefully described by the four-fold method. When
we try in preliminary fashion to define *Piers Plowman* as a whole,
we have to take into account the literal narrative of a dream-
journey, or a series of journeys: an exposition of the relationship
of Christ and man—the working of Christ in man's soul: a thorough-
going investigation of the good moral life at all levels: a record
of spiritual experience only to be compared for quality and direction
with that of the mystic.

In fact, Langland's realism, his 'literalness', draws its strength
from spirituality. And if his poem is to function properly, we must

remain conscious of this state of affairs; our reading must be at once relaxed and watchful. The allegory must be received in 'wise passiveness'; taking nothing for granted, we must demand no more in the way of conclusions and interpretations than the poetry seems willing to yield at any particular stage. Our responses must be sensitive, from the very beginning of the poem onwards, to a strongly variable depth and texture of meaning.

The first landscape which spreads out before the dreamer is of deepest symbolic import. It is the mediaeval world, with its 'universal religio-historical perspective':[1] the plain of earth, set between Heaven and Hell. It is the soul of man, watched over by God and the Devil, constantly in peril of spiritual death, in hope of spiritual life. We are launched into the dream-vision largely, seeing everything at a glance—a God's eye view—as we do in some of the great canvases of later mediaeval art. In Hieronymus Bosch's altarpiece, *The Haywain*,[2] for instance, there is the same triple arrangement of the panorama: the central panel, earth, set between a volet showing the Fall of Angels from the 'tower of truth', Heaven, and one which shows the 'deep dale of Hell' awaiting man. Religio-historical perspectives are strong here too. God broods over all, from the centre of the Heavens: the rays of light which shaft from his outstretched hands first of all rivet attention on the eternal truth which exists above and beyond all that is temporal, and then redirect attention to the seething, crowded scenes of hideous particularity below. Bosch's sinful Haywaggon grinds on through the world which is Langland's Field Full of Folk. And as in Bosch's picture the eye falls from the over-all spiritual patterning of God's purpose for man to the detailed illustration of man's ugly resistance to that purpose, so in *Piers Plowman* we soon leave one mode of allegory for another: we come down into the Field Full of Folk. For in Langland's ruthless examination of the way of the world we have not left allegory. The realism which contributes vividly to the general effect of the Prologue must not be mistaken for complete literalism. This is now allegory in a lower key, but like the central panel in Bosch's *Haywain*, it is not offered simply as a piece of documentary drawing from life .in fourteenth-century England. All these figures and groups of figures, reviewed rapidly by poet and painter, make up, and *mean* Man-on-Earth; they *mean* good and evil in the human state. Neither artist intends us

[1] Auerbach, *op. cit.*, p. 17.
[2] See Ludvig von Baldass, *Hieronymus Bosch* (London, 1960), Plates 23-5.

to forget this, just as neither intends that we forget the rays of light leading the scene back to Heaven, and the tower of truth dominating over the plain.

Within the space of thirty lines, Langland acclimatizes his reader to a flexible allegorical range which is to be his normal practice throughout the poem. Passus I, following closely upon the turbulent, realistic scenes of the prologue, is set predominantly, but not consistently, in a much richer allegorical mode. The local situation— a conversation between the dreamer and Holy Church about the opening scenes and their meaning—focuses for us a far larger situation, in which God speaks to the spirit of man through his 'vicar' on earth, the authority of the Church. The whole Passus moves subtly and easily among various sorts of significances. There is literal drama: the fumbling dreamer rebuked by the wise lady—

> 'Thow doted daffe,' quod she. 'dulle arne thi wittes;—
> To litel latyn thow lernedest. lede, in thi ȝouthe—'
>
> (B.I.138-9)

(although even at this more relaxed moment we are conscious that the poet is pointing for us the sad use man makes of his divinely created intelligence, the discrepancy between what was intended and what is). But beyond this the speech of Holy Church instructs and reveals universally; some of the most basic tenets of Christianity are given moral and mystical direction. The main theme of her discourse is the necessity of the search for and the means of attaining to Truth, to God. And this theme is never relinquished; it is conveyed, however, in a quick succession of different symbolic and spiritual modes. Behind words dealing with the way to Truth in the specific and local terms of the needs of mediaeval society—

> 'Kynges and kniȝtes. shulde kepe it bi resoun,
> Riden and rappe down. in reumes about . . .'[1]
>
> (B.I.94-5)

the long perspectives of religious history open, close and open again: the fall of the Angels, the fall of man, the sin of Cain, Lot, Judas. One vitally important record of Truth, of God's design for man, is contained in the narratives of the Bible, and Holy Church constantly returns to this source for illustrative examples. We move unquestioningly from contemporary to Biblical reference—

> 'And that is the professioun appertly. that appendeth for knyȝtes.[2] . . . .
> For Dauid in his dayes. dubbed kniȝtes . . .'
>
> (B.I.98, 102)

---

[1] '. . . ride swiftly and thoroughly about their realms . . .'
[2] '. . . and that is clearly the work which is proper to knights . . .'

and, suddenly, to reference of rarest spirituality; one line can set
the scope and aim of this quest for Truth into their highest key:
the man who walks with Truth

> '. . . is a god bi the gospel. agrounde and aloft . . .'[1]

$$(B.I.90)$$

As the Passus begins to lay greater stress upon the answer which
love provides for man in search of God, this rapid contraction and
expansion of reference becomes more marked. Contemporary
applications narrow the field of activity:

> 'For-thi I rede ʒow riche. haueth reuthe of the pouere . . .
> Many chapeleynes arne chaste. ac charite is awey . . .
> Many curatoures kepen hem. clene of here bodies,
> Thei ben acombred with coueitise . . .'

$$(B.I.173, 188, 193-4)$$

Universal statements expand it again to proportions which encompass all kinds of truth—historical, moral, mystical:

> 'Loue is leche of lyf. and nexte owre lorde selue,
> And also the graith gate. that goth in-to heuene.'

$$(B.I.202-3)$$

By the end of the Passus we are conscious that one central message
has been conveyed but on many different levels; many kinds of men,
with different vocations, are now equipped to 'seek St. Truth by
way of love'—the theme has infinite variations.

It would be impossible to study in detail the working of this
process over a wide area of the poem, but we may select for examination one very important episode—that of the Tree of Charity in
Passus XVI (B text). Langland has been criticized for the 'complex . . .
crowded'[2] allegory of this passage, and, indeed, a commentary
designed to show its entirely logical and continuous procedure,
would be a difficult task. The poetry is not 'altogether susceptible
of satisfactory rational explanation'[3] but it is generally acceptable
in terms such as we have been considering. Here, above all, Langland's allegory is conceived in many different modes, and operates
locally or globally in succession. The dreamer is pursuing his
search for the meaning of love, and Anima proposes the allegory of
the Tree of Charity. Setting out the tree by branch, leaf, flower

---

[1] See below, p. 85.   [2] Donaldson, *op. cit.*, p. 187.   [3] *Loc. cit.*

F

and fruit, the account is detailed and static; it proceeds as if it were going over a diagram, neatly labelling it:[1]

> 'Mercy is the more ther-of. the myddel stokke is Reuthe.
> The leues ben Lele-Wordes. the lawe of Holycherche.
> The blosmes beth Boxome-Speche. and Benygne-Lokynge,
> Pacience hatte the pure tre. and pore symple of herte,
> And so, thorw god and thorw good men. groweth the frute Charite.'
>
> (B.XVI.5–9)

So far the allegory is thinly dimensioned, and it continues in this way while Anima speaks didactically; the tree grows, by God's design, in the garden of man's heart, and FreeWill farms the land, under the jurisdiction of Piers the Plowman. And with the mention of Piers Plowman the allegorical 'mode' begins to change. The dreamer's delighted surprise, which reveals itself effectively by a sudden swoon of joy, and by a drop into the even deeper visionary state of a dream *within* a dream—these things should warn us that the exact continuity of the allegory has been interrupted. Piers reveals himself directly to the dreamer in this new vision, and what he says will not necessarily connect in every detail with the initial 'flat' allegory of the Tree of Charity. The idiom is changing. For now the dreamer is brought face to face with the tree by Piers; in literary terms, we are turning from plain expository allegory, to allegory of dramatic action: in spiritual, we are beginning to experience the truths already barely stated. The expansion of form and meaning is first indicated, allegorically, by the swoon and the dream within a dream—then by the dreamer's sight of the three 'props' of the Trinity which support the tree, and are Piers' weapons to ward off the attacks made upon it by the world, the flesh and the devil. Now, with the introduction of this new element (the Trinity), the larger spiritual context of qualities such as Mercy, Reuthe, Boxome-Speche, Benygne-Lokynge, Pacience and Charite begins to be made clearer; the just man is supported by all the power of God:

> *Dominus supponit manum suam*
>
> (B.XVI.26)

In the lively account of Piers' active defence of the tree, the eternal consequence of all earthly affairs is constantly brought to mind.

[1] And, in fact, Professor Bloomfield, in *Anglia*, Band 76 (1958) '*Piers Plowman* and the Three Grades of Chastity', holds that Langland's allegorical trees combine features of at least two well-known tree symbols—the Tree of Chastity and the Joachite Tree—and produces diagrammatic illustrations from mediaeval manuscripts. See further, Salter and Pearsall, *Piers Plowman*, pp. 14 foll.

So the rejection of fleshly temptations calls up the memory of Christ's passion and conquest—

> ... the passioun and the power. of owre prynce Iesu ...
>
> (B.XVI.37)

the resistance against all three, world, flesh and devil, is made 'thorw grace/And helpe of the holy goste...' (B.XVI.51-2). The allegory here is telling the dreamer how individual man struggles against evil with the help of divine examples and agencies. This analysis of the relationship of man and God in the vital problem of combating sin is already far from the diagrammatic allegory of the opening lines of the Passus. While it does not contradict anything said there, it is so much enriched in form and sense that the earlier passage, by comparison, seems barely introductory. The two exist in different—though concentric—circles of reference.

If, for instance, we try to trace exact continuity in the literal allegorical pattern, we shall find discrepancies.[1] We are first told that the blossoms on the tree are 'Boxome-Speche' and 'Benygne-Lokynge', and the leaves 'Lele-Wordes, the lawe of Holycherche' (*ll.* 6-7). Piers, when he begins to demonstrate the working of the tree, says that the Flesh, with its worms of sin, destroys the blossoms down to the bare leaves (*l.* 35). If we interpret this strictly, the meaning is curious; the temptations of the flesh are levelled against obedient speech and kind looks—all that is left after they have done their work is the bare text of God's scriptures. This is, of course, based upon a forced, out-of-context reading of the second passage. In the new allegorical context of the dream-within-a-dream, Langland has clearly moved on from the idea of the tree set in man's heart, on which 'the fruit charity' grows, to the idea of the tree of love, on which mankind—that is, man reformed in God's image—is the fruit. The two ideas are by no means antagonistic; the second is a deepened version of the first. Turning from a static to a dynamic mode, Piers describes and illustrates, in the inner dream, a process, not simply a fact: the spiritual functioning of man's soul maintained in spite of great hazards, and in response to the love of God. The blossom is no longer to be thought of as speech and looks; although it may include these things within its definition, it is now a larger concept altogether: a more advanced stage in this process of spiritual fruition which brings man to God.

---

[1] Professor Bloomfield, *op. cit.*, p. 248, note 3, records this fact: '... the tree of the dream within the dream is not exactly the same as the tree described by Anima ...' without noting the reasons for the differences.

It is very important to note how, as the allegorical idiom changes and is enriched, it begins to utilize more than one time sequence. Whereas we are conscious of a single narrative sequence in the opening description of the Tree of Charity, when Piers begins to show the dreamer how the fruit ripens on the tree we are conscious of several threads of simultaneous activity: the universal drama of God's purpose for man working out over the whole span of human history, and the divine historical events of Christ's Passion and Triumph and the coming of the Holy Ghost. This should prepare us to accept the otherwise startling transitions of the next passage: Piers' account of the different kinds of fruit on the tree (the different classes of mankind) and his shaking of the tree to illustrate further for the dreamer the nature of this fruit,[1] exist in one-time context— that of the 'continuous-present' of the dream. But this very act of shaking the tree sends us straight into the 'historical-past' of the Biblical narrative, with the falling fruit of the Old Testament gathered by the devil, and Piers, reaching out in anger with the third prop of the Trinity, the Holy Spirit, bringing about the Incarnation.[2] For many Passus to come the allegory will move in multiple time-sequences of which the Biblical narrative will be one.

Fluctuation of allegorical depth is a feature of the whole poem, but is seen here in a particularly dramatic form. At this point in *Piers Plowman* we experience, as we move from dream to inner dream, from Tree of Charity to Tree of Mankind, the passage from thin-textured allegory of local application and single dimension to subtle, multiple-time allegory of global significance and rich variety of tone. The passage is not difficult, provided we cease looking for logically patterned continuity. The direction of the allegory is not rigidly pre-determined; on the other hand, it is not a capricious progress—rather, an organic growth.

In those important respects, the nature of Langland's allegory differs from that of many other mediaeval allegories: religious works of Langland's own time, such as the *Desert of Religion* or the *Abbey of the Holy Ghost*,[3] where narrative sequence and conceptual sequence proceed consistently, and preserve the same kind of relationship to each other and to the whole poem throughout:

---

[1] *ll.* 67 foll.
[2] *ll.* 79 foll. It is interesting that Professor Bloomfield, *op. cit.*, p. 250, who is clearly looking for formal and continuous allegorical procedure in this section, sees this passage as 'a long *interlude*. . . . Langland briefly capitulates the Life and Passion of Jesus.'
[3] *Op. cit.*, above, p. 69.

secular compositions such as the *Roman de la Rose*, which functions more richly and vitally than the *Desert of Religion* and its kind, but is consistent and continuous in exactly the way *Piers Plowman* is not.[1] We should not, however, lay claim to absolute originality for *Piers Plowman* in the field of mediaeval allegorical literature. The contemporary dream-poem *Pearl*, although on a far smaller, simpler scale than *Piers Plowman*, has certain interesting points of resemblance. Reference has already been made to the similarity between the two poems in their powerful use of the 'dream-convention';[2] this similarity extends to the nature of the allegory. In both we find a relationship between allegorical narrative and concept which is rich and intimate, with the varied progress of a living and developing organism. Thus *Pearl* gives us an opening narrative of rich symbolic texture; the falling asleep, passage to the dream, journey through the dream-land and initial conversation of dreamer and Pearl-maiden not only build up dramatically to a high point of pathos and excitement, but establish a complex pattern of significances. The insistent repetition, in slightly different contexts, of the word 'pearl', for instance, means that in the dreamer's first address to the maiden who appears to him across the mysterious river

'O perle', quod I, 'in perleʒ pyʒt,[3]
Art þou my perle þat I haf playned . . .'

(*ll.* 241–2)

we move easily and strongly from local to universal applications: the pearl is, indeed, the small figure which confronts the dreamer, teasing his memory and love with the familiar looks of the earthly child now dead: she is also a vision of perfect goodness and purity, known before in part, now 'face to face'. But in the homiletic teaching then imparted to the dreamer by Pearl so that he may understand doctrinally something of the nature of the kingdom of heaven, we cease to deal with such layers of meaning; this is didactic, expository material, which will contribute to the total allegorical force of the poem, but which is, in itself, of limited symbolic

---

[1] The dangers of working from abstract definitions and neglecting literary and devotional evidence offered by the text itself, are seen in Professor Frank's division of allegory into 'symbolic' and 'personification' groups, which requires us to associate *Piers Plowman* with the *Roman de la Rose* and not with the *Divina Commedia*. (See R. W. Frank, 'The Art of Reading Mediaeval Personification—Allegory', *E.L.H.*, XX, 1953.)

[2] See above, Chapter II, p. 59.

[3] '. . . adorned with pearls . . .'

content.[1] The return to a more substantial allegorical medium begins when the pearl-maiden ends her speech, and the dreamer is *actively* involved once again in the progress of the dream. His vision of the New Jerusalem, with Christ leading the Blessed, and worshipped by all angels, is a perfect symbolic representation of the heavenly love and justice which he can now see, lying at the heart of his sorrow. The sight of Christ, joyful in spite of the great flowing wound of charity in his breast,

> Þaȝ he were hurt and wounde hade,
> In his sembelaunt watȝ neuer sene,
> So wern his glenteȝ gloryous glade.[2]

(ll. 1142–4)

points the dreamer to his own reconciliation with grief:

> 'If hit be ueray and soth sermoun
> Þat þou so stykes in garlande gay,
> So wel is me in thys doel-doungoun
> Þat þou art to that Prynseȝ paye.'[3]

(ll. 1185–8)

And his last words of dedication to Christ—

> He gef us to be his homly hyne
> Ande precious perleȝ unto his pay.

both open and close many perspectives—leading back across the whole of the poem, and even *beyond* the poem, to great Christian assumptions, universally applicable. 'Pearl' now signifies all mankind, in whom God's will and love are allowed to work, as well as one man's vision of perfection; what began as an individual's lament ends as a statement of universal responsibility.

But this variation of allegorical texture is more frequent and dramatic in *Piers Plowman*, and it is interesting that even closer analogies can be drawn between the poem and certain types of mediaeval devotional prose. The rapid variation of depth and extent of significance, the use of many different allegorical modes in close proximity, and the direction of effort to over-all wealth of meaning rather than to minute allegorical consistency are characteristic, for instance, of the influential thirteenth-century spiritual guide,

---

[1] The parable of the labourers in the vineyard, which occurs within this section, is a good example of the only kind of allegorical idiom the poet is, for the moment, prepared to use. Parable uses well-defined conceptual equivalents in its narrative: it is not vague, allusive, or particularly wide in range of application.

[2] '. . . so wonderfully happy was his expression.'

[3] 'If it is true that you are thus set in the bright garland (of the Blessed), I can endure the miserable prison (of this life) knowing you are to that Prince's pleasure.'

the *Ancrene Riwle*.[1] Its central section, on love,[2] proceeds in a way which is strongly reminiscent of *Piers Plowman*—moving without explanation from one kind of allegorical writing into another. Beginning with a general statement on love, we pass to the allegory of the lady wooed by a king (the soul wooed by Christ). And first of all the whole episode is covered quickly—an allegorical outline of Christ's coming, the love-letters written with his own blood as a proof of devotion.[3] Then comes a more detailed, deepened treatment of the matter; we are taken back over the story of the king's wooing, his speeches, gifts, actions, and his death, in terms of dynamic, not static allegory.[4] So in *Piers Plowman* we passed from the brief outline of the Tree of Charity to the dramatic demonstration of its nature by Piers himself. The *Ancrene Riwle* author then changes his approach once more. Concentrating on the shield of Christ, he works at it as a symbol, extracting all possible sorts of significances out of its shape, material and function; we are back with allegory of a static and, now, pictorial kind. After this, the main continuity of allegorical theme is interrupted; although 'theo luve thet iesu crist haueth to his deore leofmon',[5] is still the subject, new allegorical ideas are introduced to define it—mother-love, the blood-bath, the knotted girdle[6]—and it is some little time before we return to the original metaphor of the 'wooing of our Lord'. But when we do in the last speech which Christ makes to the soul,[7] the allegory is many-voiced; we are asked to respond not to an allegorical diagram, narrative or dramatic excerpt, but to a speech of moving symbolic reference, morally and mystically powerful.

This kind of progression is not unusual. Other parts of the work illustrate even more vividly how writers such as these, while providing an allegorical framework for a passage or section, do not hesitate to improvise, even to the point of dislocating that framework, if a greater spiritual suggestiveness can be achieved thereby. In an earlier section the anchoress is likened to a bird flying up to heaven, and the idea of the aspiration of the anchoress forms the theme of an extensive passage.[8] But the allegory is elaborated without scrupulous regard for an entirely accurate build-up of detail; the basic concepts are developed continuously but the allegory itself may disregard continuity in the interests of immediate aptness and vigour. So, at the beginning of the passage, the wings

[1] Ed. M. Day (E.E.T.S., O.S. 225, 1952).   [2] *Ibid.*, p. 176 foll.   [3] *Ibid.*, p. 177.
[4] *Ibid.*, pp. 177-9.   [5] *Ibid.*, p. 179: '. . . the love which Christ has for his dear beloved.'
[6] *Ibid.*, p. 180.   [7] *Ibid.*, p. 181.   [8] *Ibid.*, p. 57 foll.

which bear the anchoress upwards in flight are her good habits, resulting in good works: by the end of the passage, good works are represented by the young birds which are brought forth by the anchoress in her nest. Similar 'difficulties' have been met with in Langland's allegorical practice; while the general theme goes forward, the allegory is allowed freest action—the two trees of Passus XVI are not, in fact, identical in every detail, but they are inseparably joined at the liferoots of their meaning.

This loose, rich allegorical procedure is employed by many of the writers of spiritual treatises nearer Langland's own day and it seems very likely that here, rather than in any poetic work, we should look for the immediate background to the allegorical procedure of *Piers Plowman*. When Walter Hilton, in the *Scale of Perfection*, turns to allegory for a prolonged period, he manages it similarly to Langland. The pilgrimage to Jerusalem, in Book II, is an allegory of variable nature, which is sometimes engaged at full spiritual and symbolic pressure, working consistently and harmoniously on both narrative and conceptual levels:

And if thou wilt hold this way, and do as I have said, I undertake thy life that thou shalt not be slain, but that thou shalt come to that place that thou covetest. (Chapter 21)

but which sometimes, in mid-course, draws upon new and slighter allegorical imaginings: the pilgrim is seen as an empty vessel,[1] as a man setting sticks to the inner fire of devotion.[2] It also introduces commentary which is intrinsically non-allegorical, but which contributes generally to the total allegorical meaning. Although both the *Ancrene Riwle* and the *Scale of Perfection*, having specific function as guides to the spiritual life, differ in some important ways from *Piers Plowman*, all three are of varied allegorical texture; fruitful, rather than accurately and consistently charted significance, is their aim. Something of the same nature has already been observed of *Pearl*, and it is interesting that there, too, a fluctuating allegorical procedure follows a movement between vision and sermon which is a familiar feature of the spiritual prose treatises. The links between all these works are obvious if we compare them with any religious (or secular) allegory of strict practice. What we find in the latter (of which, it has been suggested, the *Desert of Religion* and the *Abbey of the Holy Ghost* are

---

[1] *Op. cit.*, p. 307.   [2] *Ibid.*, p. 309.

good examples) provides the strongest contrast: shallow, single-toned diagrammatic allegory, in which the metaphorical elements have exact conceptual equivalents, and in which the author is never distracted from a central purpose because he has a limited amount of material to convey.

It appears that, for allegorical usages as for basic material and structural elements, *Piers Plowman* represents a synthesis of much that is traditional in mediaeval art and thought. We cannot rule out the possible influence of the 'four-levelled' mode of interpretation upon Langland's approach to his subject; on the other hand, his manipulation of allegory reminds us less of the exact methods of mediaeval exegesis than of the free and flexible procedures of some manuals dealing comprehensively with the spiritual life.[1]

(ii) *The Meaning of the Allegory*

It has already been proposed that what makes *Piers Plowman* so much more than 'the quintessence of English mediaeval preaching' is its existence within the context of not simply a dream, but a vision, and now that we come to consider the intention of Langland's allegory we are again led, for elucidation and commentary, away from purely homiletic literature towards writings of higher spirituality which can encompass both sermon and vision.

If, on first consideration, the probability of finding much common ground for *Piers Plowman* and such treatises seems remote, we should remember that the distance between mystical and other kinds of devotional literature in the later Middle Ages was much smaller than might be supposed. Works intended to have widest range of application could, nevertheless, draw upon doctrines and experiences of the rarest sort

þe whiche man may not, ne kan not, speke . . .[2]

Manuals professedly concerned with contemplation often also provided teaching of the staple moral kind so familiar in the mediaeval sermon: on the virtues, the vices, the commandments, the Lord's prayer. That mediaeval man at this period felt the essential unity (though not necessarily the complete accessibility) of the

---

[1] Compare the remark of Dr. J. A. W. Bennett, *The Listener*, XLIII, No. 1101 (1950), p. 381: 'Allegory is not a literary method so much as a way of embodying a spiritual truth.'

[2] *The Cloud of Unknowing, op. cit.*, p. 62. Nothing is known about the station and life of this writer—but his authorship of several treatises on contemplative prayer has now been established by Prof. Hodgson in her edition of *The Cloud* and of *Deonise Hid Divinite* (E.E.T.S., O.S. 231, 1955).

whole area of religious experience, from the analysis and correction of sin to the 'ghostly sight' of God's mysteries, is well proved by many texts available during Langland's lifetime. The *Mirror* of St. Edmund of Canterbury,[1] an originally thirteenth-century work which had powerful influence in the following century, contains the usual homiletic matter, as well as vivid meditations upon the Life and Passion of Christ, and discussion of how to 'luke one . . . godde in his awene kynde',[2] Walter Hilton's *Scale of Perfection*,[3] contemporary with *Piers Plowman*, treats dramatically with the deadly sins as well as with the 'privy voice of Jhesu sounding in a soul'.[4] In fact, as a recent writer has reminded us,

> . . . the writings of the mystics and the religious lyrics of the fourteenth century . . . are also connected, more closely than might be expected . . . with the moral treatises, and even with the instructions for priests.[5]

Richard Rolle, perhaps the most famous of all mediaeval English mystics,[6] has much in his Epistles, addressed to a contemplative, of general moral import; moreover, he composed a treatise for use by parish priests in their more everyday duties.

All evidence points towards the conclusion that didactic and mystical literature were connected, at this time, in a firmly orthodox manner. Many writers were engaged on interpreting high spiritual states for those perhaps not capable of direct personal knowledge. Nicholas Love's *Mirror of the Blessed Life of Jesu Christ* has staple narrative information and didactic comment; it is also strongly preoccupied with affective meditation, such as that which the Middle Ages saw as the preliminary to the highest state of grace,[7] and hints at the author's own attainment to that state.[8] The *Mirror* was owned by all classes of readers during the fifteenth century, and illustrates once more the comprehensive nature of these later mediaeval books which were often designed for the needs of the

---

[1] The *Speculum Ecclesiae*, written before 1240: various English versions exist—the earliest made about 1350. C. Horstman edits two versions in *Yorkshire Writers*, I. 219 foll.

[2] *Op. cit.*, p. 239.

[3] *Op. cit.* above. Numerous MSS. were in circulation during the fourteenth and fifteenth centuries: it had a wide and enduring influence.

[4] *Op. cit.*, p. 451.

[5] W. A. Pantin, *The English Church in the Fourteenth Century* (Cambridge, 1955), p. 191.

[6] For his life and writings, see H. E. Allen, *English Writings of Richard Rolle* (Oxford, 1931).

[7] See E. Gilson, *The Mystical Theology of St. Bernard*, pp. 79–80: '. . . the place occupied in Cistercian mysticism by the meditation on the visible humanity of Christ . . . is but a beginning, but an absolutely necessary beginning. . . . For it cannot indeed be doubted that sensitive devotion to the Person of Christ will be rewarded with clearly marked mystical states . . .'

[8] *The Mirror*, pp. 208–9.

devout lay parson as well as for those of the religious.[1] In such works, the heights of the spiritual life remain in view even when the main activity takes place on a fairly unambitious level; mystical references are not felt to be eccentric or inappropriate.

The recognition that mediaeval mystical literature has its roots in the firm dogmatic teaching of the Church, that didactic, meditative and mystical content is frequently found in natural sequence within the scope of a single text, bears instantly upon *Piers Plowman*.[2] Laying claim, as it does, from almost the opening lines, to a rich area of potential significance, it may easily touch upon issues which the later Middle Ages did not regard as the exclusive preserve of a certain class and mind. With the most important of its organizing principles adapted from the practice of the mediaeval pulpit, and a strong predilection for exactly those themes and images through which the preachers of the day exhorted men to 'do wel', it transcends sermon as often as it returns to it. Whether Langland was consciously working with four-levelled allegory or not, he was certainly conforming to an accepted devotional pattern in this two-way movement.

It is not surprising, therefore, that some of Langland's deeper meanings can be more fruitfully 'glossed' by mystical than by homiletic literature.

Texts such as Walter Hilton's *Scale of Perfection* and *The Cloud of Unknowing* can often increase understanding of Langland's dramatic symbolism. We witness, for instance, how Piers the Plowman, a humble worker, leads all others on the pilgrimage to Truth with his doctrine of love, and we watch spiritual life growing in him as the poem progresses. Moreover, not only does his spiritual stature increase over the length of the poem: he stands, at its climax, to represent the divine element in man, the Christ element, and at its conclusion, to represent the truth of God reposed in man.

This miraculous transformation which inspires the dramatic and challenging words '*Petrus, id est, Christus*',[3] is, in fact, a familiar mystical concept—the growth of the divine in ordinary man

---

[1] See Pantin, *op. cit.*, pp. 253 onwards, for comment upon the 'rise of the devout layman'.

[2] The failure to see this vitiates critical studies as widely separated in time and approach as Miss Greta Hort's *Piers Plowman and Contemporary Religious Thought* (Cambridge, 1937) in which (p. 158) she distinguishes the mystical, heretical-theological, and orthodox-theological movements of the fourteenth century, placing Langland firmly in the third class, and Professor R. W. Frank's more recent study, *Piers Plowman and the Scheme of Salvation*, which is convinced that 'the poet's vision is . . . realistic rather than mystical' (p. 118).

[3] B.XV.206.

brought about by grace. The *Cloud* author describes simply and directly how

> oure soule, bi vertewe of þis reformyng grace, is mad sufficient at þe fulle to comprehende al him by loue. . . . þe eendles merueilous miracle of loue, þe whiche schal neuer take eende . . . (pp. 18–19)

The struggle to 'comprehende al him by loue' is, in fact, the major activity of the poem: worked out on ranging spiritual levels, it is, at its highest and most mysterious in Piers himself, an examination of a relationship with God comparable to that of the mystic.

A bare statement of the gist of the poem makes it clear that Langland is concerned with illuminative as well as with moral and satirical processes. The opening Prologue and Passus I lay out and define the field of action: Earth, the Field Full of Folk, lying between the valley, Hell, and the castle on a hill-top, Heaven. Truth, who is God, dwells in this castle. The first pilgrimage is that recommended to the repentant by Reason in Passus V, and led by the plowman, Piers: the pilgrimage to St. Truth. And although, in fact, Piers never leads these particular pilgrims on their way, the search for truth of all kinds, but above all, the search for the supreme Truth—God—becomes the dominant theme of the poem.[2] The successive searches for Dowel, Dobet and Dobest, which occupy the main sections of the poem[3] are parts of this great general pilgrimage; Piers is always leading dreamer and reader, as they pursue their roads to Truth. We may lose sight of our guide for long periods, but we hear of him; the dreamer struggles after him, fainting for joy at the mere sound of his name. Moreover, Piers undergoes changes on his journey to Truth, and is met with, transfigured; without ever abandoning completely his familiar 'plowman humanity', he comes to be understood in terms of the highest spiritual authority—in those of love and truth. He is in closest, most intimate connection with Christ and the Holy Spirit, and at the end of the poem, he is sought for as St. Truth was, at the beginning.

If we take this narrative seriously, as it develops and deepens, we are forced to believe that Langland intends far more than just an investigation of sin, the good Christian life, even of salvation.[4]

---

[1] See 'Medieval Poetry and the Figural View of Reality', *op. cit.*, for further comment upon the nature and function of Piers.

[2] See below, pp. 96 foll.

[3] Passus VIII–XV, XVI–XVIII, XIX–XX of the B text, respectively, according to the manuscript rubrics.

[4] Cf. Frank, *op. cit.*, p. 118: salvation is the poem's 'reason for being'.

In this poem, many aims drive towards, and are fulfilled, in one major conclusion: the dreamer does learn 'the truth' about good and evil, and salvation, but he learns in process of discovering how, through love, man is able to reach the Truth, which is God. Here the mystics are of service: it is not that Langland cannot be understood without them—rather, they help us to the full richness of his meaning. Their writings are concerned with the journey to St. Truth; they meditate upon, and *experience*, those very processes by which the simplest plowman can, in God's grace, be transformed and come to recognize divinity within himself. Piers, as all the mystics know, intuitively and by revelation, can partake of what is divine; can, if the symbolic nature of the language be admitted, 'become a God'. St. Bernard, whose writings, directly or indirectly, strongly influenced English mystical thought, had already made this clear in the twelfth century; the mystical rapture, by reforming the soul to the likeness of God, can be said to deify it:

Sic affici, deificari est[1]

Langland's English contemporary, the author of *The Cloud*, is similarly emphatic:

. . . bi his mercy wiþouten þi desert arte (thou) maad a God in grace, onyd wiþ him in spirit wiþ-outen departyng, boþe here & in blis of heuen wiþouten any eende. So þat, þouȝ þou be al one wyþ hym in grace, ȝit þou arte ful fer bineþe hym in kynde . . . (p. 120)

The metaphor of the pilgrimage, in which Langland sets both the process of change undergone by Piers and the dreamer's gradual comprehension of that process, is used significantly by Walter Hilton in the *Scale*. His development of the metaphor to describe the soul seeking God is, at times, extremely close to that of Langland, emphasizing and clarifying the main flow of Langland's allegory and, in particular, the much-debated figure of Piers. The pilgrim of the *Scale* wishes to set out for Jerusalem, but has to ask the way:

There was a man that would go to Jerusalem; and for he knew not the way he came to another man that he hoped knew the way thither, and asked whether he might come to that city.

(Book II, Chapter 21)

[1] *De diligendo Deo*, X. ed. J. P. Migne, *P.L.* CLXXXII. 991: 'Thus to be affected is to become a god.' Cf. the line quoted above (p. 73): the man who walks with Truth is 'a god bi the gospel' (B.I.90).

So the crowd of pilgrims in *Piers Plowman*, after repenting of their sins, are determined to seek St. Truth, but

> . . . there was wyȝte non so wys. the wey thider couthe,
> But blustreden forth as bestes. ouer bankes and hilles . . .
>
> (B.V.520–1)   1)

until Piers comes on the scene and offers to lead them:

> 'Ac if ȝe wilneth to wende wel. this is the weye thider,
> That I shal say to yow. and sette yow in the sothe.'
>
> (BV. 568–9)

The guide in the *Scale* gives directions to Jerusalem which correspond in general terms to those of Piers. The difficulty of the way is not to be underestimated:

> . . . he might not come thither without great trouble and mickle travail, for the way is long and perils are great of thieves and robbers . . .
>
> (Book II, Chapter 21)

It begins painfully in repentance and expiation of sins, in submission to the laws of Holy Church:

> 'The beginning of the high way in the which thou shalt go is reforming in faith, grounded meekly in the faith and in the laws of Holy Kirk . . . if thou be now reformed by the sacrament of penance after the law of Holy Kirk, . . . thou art in the right way.'   (*Ibid.*)

Piers also sets down, as the first stages of the journey, meekness, a clear conscience, and obedience to the commandments of the Church:

> 'Ȝe mote go thourgh Mekenesse. bothe men and wyues,
> Tyl ȝe come in-to Conscience. that Cryst wite the sothe. . . .
> And so boweth forth bi a broke. Beth-buxum-of-speche,
> Tyl ȝe fynden a forth. ȝowre-fadres-honoureth,
>   *Honora patrem et matrem, etc.*'[1]
>
> (B.V.570 foll. In the lines which follow, all of the Commandments are dealt with.)

After these preliminaries, the way lies straight ahead: Hilton writes then of what will sustain the traveller:

> Now then, since thou art in the sure way, if thou wilt speed in thy going and make good journeys thee behoveth to hold these two things often in thy mind: meekness and love. . . . Meekness saith, I am nought, I have nought. Love saith, I covet nought but one, and that is Jhesu . . .
>
> (Book II, Chapter 21)

---

[1] 'Men and women, you must go through Meekness, till you come to Conscience—and there may Christ guide you truly. And so travel on along by a brook, Obedient-Speech, till you reach a ford, Honour-Your-Parents . . .' The whole passage is quoted above, p. 32.

Piers also knows that no pilgrim can come to the court of Truth without the help of Christ and Mary:

'. . . thoru3e the helpe of hem two.(hope thow none other),
Thow my3te gete grace there.bi so thow go bityme.'[1]

(B.V.646–7)

and throughout the poem constant stress is laid on the necessity of moving towards Truth, or towards God, by means of charity and humility:

'Loue is leche of life.and next owre lorde selue,
And also the graith gate.that goth in-to heuene.'

(B.I.202–3)

In fact, both Hilton and Langland are dealing with similar spiritual processes, although Langland, writing for a wide audience and not, as Hilton, for a specialized contemplative order, provides for more than one level of application. His pilgrimage will serve for all men, whatever their business and capabilities.

The function and nature of Piers himself also becomes clearer in some respects by reference to this section of the *Scale*. The man who gives directions to Hilton's pilgrim has great spiritual authority; although at one point he claims that he has never reached Jerusalem ('though it be so that I were never there . . .' Book II, Chapter 21) yet at other times he speaks with the warm certainty of Christ:

That other man answers and says thus: 'Lo, I set thee in the right way. This is the way, and that thou keep the lesson that I teach thee. . . . And if thou wilt hold this way and do as I have said, I undertake thy life that thou shalt not be slain, but thou shalt come to that place that thou covetest.' (*Ibid.*)

So Piers, on his first entry into the poem, a simple plowman, has some knowledge of spiritual mysteries; not only does he tell the listening pilgrims of the way to the court of St. Truth, of God, but also describes its nature, what will be there at the journey's end. When they have travelled the long and difficult road, they will find, he says, St. Truth within their hearts:[2] the divine within the travelling human pilgrim. A man who can say this with such assurance is no ordinary well-informed son of Holy Church; from these words we might hope and even expect some later revelation about his form and function. The seeds of spiritual growth are already in Piers when he first enters the poem, and no transformation

[1] 'Through their help—do not expect any other—you can obtain grace (to reach) there, if you set out early enough.' [2] B.V.615–16.

should surprise reader or dreamer. When we read in the *Scale*
that, whoever the first instructor was, the figure who leads the
pilgrim all the way to Truth is Christ himself, it seems natural,
almost inevitable, that Langland should gradually expand the significance of Piers to Christ-figure, who encompasses human and
divine. Piers continues to lead the Pilgrimage to Truth (though
the pilgrims are now not the blustering crowd he originally came
to help, but reader and dreamer) just as Christ leads Hilton's pilgrim
to God:

... Behold Him well, for He goeth before thee, not in bodily likeness, but un-
seeably by privy presence of His might. ... He shall lead thee in the right way
to Jerusalem. ...

(*Scale*, Book II, Chapter 24)

So, in the second large section of the poem (Passus VIII–XV)
the transfigured Piers—transfigured in that Langland is now con-
tinually defining him as love, and once as Christ himself—dominates
the scene even when absent 'in bodily likeness'. The dreamer,
amidst all the confusion of people and situations, reaches out to
Piers as the answer to and the goal of all his searchings:

'Piers the Plowman!' quod I tho. and al for pure ioye
That I herd nempne his name. anone I swouned after ...

(B.XVI.18–19)

The changing part played by Piers in the allegory is, indeed,
illuminated by Hilton's words on Christ. Christ, he says, does
everything in this journeying. He inspires the pilgrim to set out,
he tells him of the means of travel, he goes in front of him on the
way, and he is, most important, the long-desired end of the journey:

... He maketh this desire in thee and He giveth it thee, and He it is that desireth
in thee, and He it is that is desired. He is all, and He doth all, if thou might see
Him.[1]

(*Scale*, Book II, Chapter 24)

Langland displays this same idea to us, but in dramatic, moving
allegory; Piers becomes the comprehensive symbol for the varied
operation of Christ in man's soul. Hilton *tells* us of the process;
Langland *shows* it to us in action. For Piers, while he certainly
stands, as the poem unfolds, for Christ the instructor, Christ the
lover, Christ the receiver of the soul, always retains some of the

[1] Compare Chapter XXVI of the *Revelations* of Dame Julian of Norwich: 'I it
am, I it am ... I it am that thou lovest, I it am that thou enjoyest, I it am that thou servest,
I it am that thou longest for ... I it am that showed me here to thee.'

endearing familiar characteristics of the plowman, the human being to whom all these miraculous things happen by grace: 'a reasonable instrument wherein that He (Christ) worketh' (*Scale, ibid.*). He is always, to some extent, Hilton's simple pilgrim on the road to Jerusalem as well as 'the man that he hoped knew the way thither' and 'He . . . that is desired'.[1]

Here Hilton and Langland deal, in their own characteristic ways, with an issue which was of primary importance in mediaeval religious thought. None of the other English mystics use the metaphor of the pilgrimage as exactly as Hilton,[2] but they all agree on the essentials of this search for Jerusalem, or St. Truth, or God: divine love creates in man the aspiration to journey towards God, but it also provides the only means of travel—love.[3]

> . . . By loue may he be getyn & holdyn; bot bi þought neiþer.
> (*Cloud*, p. 26).

The answer given to the woman contemplative, Dame Julian of Norwich, after fifteen years of meditation upon her visions, would serve Langland's dreamer too, as he works painfully towards *his* revelations:

> Wouldst thou learn thy Lord's meaning in this thing? Learn it well: Love was his meaning. Who shewed it thee? Love. What shewed He thee? Love. Wherefore shewed it He? For Love. Hold thee therein and thou shalt learn and know more in the same. But thou shalt never know nor learn therein other thing without end.
>
> (*Revelations*, Chapter LXXXVI)

So also, these writings, not Miracle Play, Religious History or Sermon, give us most help in understanding the final phases of Langland's poem: the dramatic drop from the exalted vision of the Crucifixion and Harrowing of Hell to the workaday vision of this world, the sinful Field Full of Folk, where the search for holiness,

---

[1] E. Gilson, *op. cit.*, p. 128, writing of the Bernardian mystical 'metamorphosis' of man as he searches for oneness with God has this to say:
'To eliminate from self all that stands in the way of being really oneself, that is not to lose but to find oneself once more.'
So Piers is not altered out of all recognition, but revealed in perfected form. Compare St. Bernard, *De Diligendo Deo, loc. cit.*, 'Manebit quidem substantia, sed in alia forma, alia gloria, aliaque potentia'. For a more detailed examination of this theme, see the article by the present writer, 'Piers Plowman and the Pilgrimage to Truth', *Essays and Studies* (1958).

[2] Dame Julian does say, in Chapter LXXXI of the *Revelations*, concerning Christ's showing of himself to man 'He shewed Himself in earth thus as it were in pilgrimage: that is to say, He is here with us, leading us, and shall be till when He Hath brought us all to His bliss in heaven'.

[3] Compare Gilson, *op. cit.*, p. 149:
'. . . what is it that transforms the soul to the likeness of God? Charity, love, and nothing else.'

G

truth, God, must begin all over again. Dame Julian says vividly
that the desire and the search for God are never finished; there is
no absolute resting in God for the mystic, even after communion
has taken place. What happens is that he or she is given increased
spiritual power to help others, and to set out on the pilgrimage
once more:

> And thus I saw Him, and sought Him; and I had Him, I wanted Him.
>
> > *(Revelations,* Chapter X)

The recurring pilgrimage of *Piers Plowman,* the constant finding
and losing which culminates in the great loss of Piers in the final
Passus—all of this is a familiar part of the spiritual life as it is known
to the mystics. After illumination, there is new work to be done,
not only within the self, but, in a practical way, on the Field Full of
Folk.[1] As the mystic is reconciled to the passage from spiritual
ecstasy to the normal busy world of religious experience, so, by
imaginative projection, the poet Langland knows that the splendid
vision of divine love, suffering and triumphant, must be followed
by the pilgrimage to rediscover, to re-interpret what has been seen
for the sake of humanity and for the sake of the individual soul.

   But if our comprehension of the allegory is widened and deepened
by a knowledge of these spiritual writings, we should not neglect
to consider how carefully it is guided by Langland throughout
the poem itself. He provides for our understanding in several
most important ways—using, firstly, the constantly renewed motif
of a journey. We are searching for something, somebody, from the
beginning of the allegory, are involved in a series of pilgrimages,
and start out again in the last lines. During the whole of our
reading we are being reminded of the activity proper to poet,
dreamer and reader—that of journeying. When we are reconciled
to this unceasing movement, and can accept exploration almost as an
end in itself, then we are in a fit state to receive, perhaps at most
unexpected moments, the fruits of exploration. The need to endure
along humble and apparently unrewarding paths, if we are to come

---

[1] Evelyn Underhill, in Chapter X of *Mysticism* (London, 1923) discusses this passage
between 'action and fruition' as particularly characteristic of Western spirituality. Her
quotation, p. 522, from the writing of the Dutch contemplative Ruysbroeck (1293–1381)
which describes the state in which the mystic both rests in God and works for others in the
world of affairs has a powerful relevance to the renewed activity at the end of *Piers Plowman:*
   '. . . God, in his communications, incessantly compels him to renew both this rest and this
work . . . He is active in all loving work, for he sees his rest. He is a pilgrim, for he sees his
country. Thus this man . . . goes towards God by inward love, in eternal work, and he
goes in God by his fruitful inclination in eternal rest. And he dwells in God; and yet he
goes out towards created things in a spirit of love towards all things.'

to wisdom, is firmly impressed upon the dreamer many times—most strikingly in Passus XI, where first Christ is pictured journeying with man:

> 'For owre ioye and owre hele. Iesu Cryst of heuene,
> In a pore mannes apparaille. pursueth vs euere,
> And loketh on vs in her liknesse. and that with louely chere . . .'
>   (B.XI.179–81)

and then God:

> '. . . for pylgrymes ar we alle;
> And in the apparaille of a pore man. and pilgrymes lyknesse
> Many tyme god hath ben mette . . .'
>   (B.XI.234–6)

For the dreamer and those travelling with him, the coming to answers, the meeting with truth, wisdom, God, will not take place by demand, but only by the most patient, undemanding search.

Secondly, we are given a poet-dreamer. This is vital from the point of view of art and sense. While the poet himself may have a grasp of essential meaning, retain a bird's-eye view of the courses of thought and narrative as they wind towards conclusions, the dreamer is uninformed. He can, therefore, be used for the sake of the reader,[1] to display meaning in all its subtlety and complexity. He stumbles, hesitates, protests when all seems obscure:

> This is a longe lessoun . . . and litel am I the wyser . . .

appeals to the various figures he meets:

> 'Kenne me bi somme crafte. to knowe . . .'

and is impelled to travel, question, put his ideas together—somewhat feebly at times—only to be rebuffed and humiliated for his lack of understanding:

> 'Thow doted daffe . . . dulle arne thi wittes . . .'

The dreamer, 'in the mase' as we are, is the strongest possible link between us, and the meaning of the allegory. Langland's meaning is expounded through his fumbling mind, and we, reassured by the simple familiarity of the situation, are able to share in his growing comprehension. The device of the dreamer, used well in poems as diverse as the *Book of the Duchess*, *Pearl* and *Piers*

---

[1] For the sake of the poet, too, perhaps? Although Langland is in command of main ideas, it seems that the dreamer does often represent his own unformed, even uncertain, meditation on those ideas.

Plowman, ensures in a dramatic and responsible way that the reader plays an integral part in the unravelling of the allegory: he cannot ever be more stupid than the man who dreams.[1]

Then, too, we are told a great deal about Langland's intentions by listening carefully to the poetry itself. As we have seen, the fact that his art is controlled by a spiritual rather than an aesthetic force is an added persuasion towards attending closely to rhythmic flow, sound patterning and image: his poetry serves his purposes in a particularly intimate manner. And so the discovery of likenesses in material and method between Langland's allegory and other mediaeval works does not imply that they are to be read and interpreted in *exactly* the same way, with identical placing of emphases: the graph of meaning may not be identically curved.

For instance, the nature and quality of some of the poetry in the third section (B. Passus XVI–XVIII) indicate to us, if nothing else does, that a climax, both artistic and spiritual, has been reached. At this stage the positive revelation of God's love is made to the dreamer; what happens after this section (Passus XIX–XX) happens on a lower level. Then exultation is replaced by the impulse towards active organization; the Church is set to work to utilize for all men the fruits of vision. Thoughtfulness, concern for practical religious issues, disillusionment, reinforcement of hope, are all expressed in a poetry which is admirably equipped for its task, but which is clearly of a lower tension than that of Christ's speeches after the Harrowing of Hell. The poetic graph here follows and is a guide to a spiritual charting; the rhythm is unmistakeable. Considering this, it is strange that such determined efforts are made to find patterns of meaning in *Piers Plowman* which ignore this natural rhythm. One recent proposal of the three Bernardian stages of the spiritual life, humility, charity, unity, as a possible thematic progression for the poem,[2] has much that is suggestive in it, but it will not fit exactly into parts II, III, and IV of the work; the writer's failure to adjust 'unity' to part IV is indicative not—as he concludes—that 'the poem stopped short of its goal' but that, if this particular scheme was in Langland's mind at all, it was formulated in a different way. 'Unity', the achievement of a perfect accord with, and an experience of, the love of God, does belong to the poem—although not in the same exclusively mystical terms as St. Bernard uses. It belongs, however,

---

[1] Mediaeval allegory of this kind has a far better chance of being understood than Renaissance allegory (Spenser's, for instance). There is no need for footnotes to mediaeval fables; the dreamer himself is the gloss.

[2] See Donaldson, *op. cit.,* pp. 196 foll.

to part III of *Piers Plowman*, where the goal is reached, for the dreamer, by participation in a vision divinely bestowed. 'Unity' and 'charity' are here demonstrated and experienced as inseparable parts of a whole, not as stages in a progress towards perfection. The same sort of preoccupation with a spiritual ordering which is similar but not identical to that of Langland, leads another critic to see in the last part of the work a deliberate departure from a norm otherwise accepted by the poet; moving, as he thinks, towards a climax in the last few Passus, 'the mystical stage in which the Holy Ghost works unimpeded in the soul', Langland instead turns aside to 'the life of Prelates', the building up of the structure of the Church.[1] In fact, the 'unimpeded working' of the Holy Ghost, or of Christ, in man's soul has been dramatically illustrated on various levels by the whole of the third section, in which Piers and Christ are seen to operate as a single, invincible force, and the dreamer is reconciled at last to the lesson of love he was so slow to understand. Once we stop trying to equate the stages of the poem with any particular mediaeval system, and learn (among other things, of course) from the verse itself how Langland modified and manipulated for his own purposes what he received, then we are in less danger of making narrow or misplaced judgements of those purposes.

A 'poetic' reading of *Piers Plowman* contributes notably towards our interpretation of Piers himself. Langland obviously used all his artistry to make us attend to Piers—the management of his first entry, vivid, unexpected, gives us a lead we are never allowed to drop. The authority as well as the attractiveness of this figure are impressed upon us by lively writing during the busy scenes of B. Passus I–VII. But the process does not end here. If we listen sympathetically to the poetry of the later Passus, it is clearly telling us of the increasingly powerful function and meaning of Piers; we can ignore the *mystery* of Piers' development only if we ignore the poetry, and the careful positioning of the poetry, by which it is conveyed. The progress of the exploratory, discursive second part of the poem (B. Passus VIII–XV) is pointed by references to the absent Piers, made in commanding poetry—poetry which is undeniably meant to stand out from its more ordinary surroundings and build up a sense of urgent expectancy in dreamer and reader:

---

[1] Professor T. P. Dunning, 'The Structure of the B-Text of *Piers Plowman*', *R.E.S.*, N.S. VII (1956). His assumptions lead him to a very limited interpretation of Piers at the end of the poem—Conscience departs in search of a 'true Pope' (p. 237).

> For one Pieres the Ploughman.hath impugned vs alle,
> And sette alle sciences at a soppe.saue loue one . . .
> Thanne passe we ouer til Piers come.and preue this in dede . . .
>
> (B.XIII.123–4, 132)
>
> And that knoweth no clerke.ne creature in erthe,
> But Piers the Plowman.*Petrus, id est, Christus* . . .
>
> (B.XV.205–6)

The high point is reached in Passus XVI, when the dreamer, faced with the great Tree of Charity, swoons at the very mention of Piers, and is immediately brought into a vision of the highest spiritual import. He does not wake from this 'lone dreme' until he has seen, through the agency of Piers, that 'love is his meaning'. The placing of the artistic emphases is calculated to impress upon us how, if we follow Piers, we are moving from inquiry to revelation; the literary-dramatic form expresses the growth, and, at the same time, the penetration of a mystery:

> . . . and atte laste me thouȝte,
> That Pieres the Plowman.al the place me shewed . . .
>
> (B.XVI.20–1)

In the B text, certainly, by means of boldly set poetry, a general rhythm which swings from suspense to relief of suspense, a succession of exciting, unexpected appearances and disappearances, Langland forces us to enlarge our conception of what Piers may signify. Whatever doctrinal difficulties may be produced by such a process of enlargement,[1] we are not justified in disregarding the poetic signs which tell us plainly of urgent and high intentions.

Finally, in our search for these 'high intentions', the poem's 'reason for being', we must avoid over-complicating the issues, recognizing that Langland's basic themes, though capable of wide spiritual development, are often in essence extremely familiar and straightforward. His manipulation of them does, at first sight, create an impression of tremendous complexity—an impression which is revealed as false when once we have grasped the nature of his allegorical procedures and his characteristic method of stating, and restating themes, situations, concepts in slightly different variations, with continuous verbal link and echo. The debate, the investigation of his themes may, indeed, lead to subtle and complex discussion, but Langland returns again and again to help us with the clear avowal of doctrine or belief. The final impression is of

---

[1] Difficulties, for instance, which seem to have persuaded him to remove certain of the more audacious lines of the B text in the C revision. See Appendix.

a positive and direct nature. So the poem demonstrates to us faith, no more and no less deep than that contained in 'Pater Noster' and 'Fiat Voluntas Tua', but demonstrates also the whole winding hinterland to faith. And this hinterland is explored through an individual mind, an individual's struggle to understand and accept the Christian world of birth, death and resurrection, the salvation of man by the sacrifice of love. The basic structure of the thematic progression of the poem is comparatively simple; it takes the form of a series of statements or propositions, set out plainly, inquired into, illustrated, and then set out again and again, gathering weight and authority at each successive inquiry. It is true that the convictions which Langland has at the end of *Piers Plowman* are no more unusual or profound than those with which he started out. But he has, in his dreamer, travelled the full circle of thought and feeling necessary to *understand* them, and we have shared in the experience. The journey lies through the confusion of the world, of the mind, and of the whole creation, and it returns to the starting-point with the same faith, but with deeper comprehension:

> And the end of all our exploring
> Will be to arrive where we started
> And know the place for the first time.

The end is, in fact, foretold at the beginning, and no less at various resting places along the way. We are given our guides to meaning and intention, even our conclusions, very early on in the poem; it may be, however, that we do not at first 'know the place', do not recognize them as such.

In many ways, the Prologue and Passus I of the poem tell us almost all we need to know about Langland's basic material, approach and conclusions. The Prologue gives us first a bird's-eye view of the whole of Earth, Heaven and Hell; it then narrows down to the Field Full of Folk, and we see

> ... alle maner of men. the mene and the riche,
> Worchyng and wandryng. as the worlde asketh.
>   (B.Prol.18–19)

Here is the satirical, realistic material with which the poet starts—the point of departure. It is a grim scene, and Langland's attitude to it is condemnatory; his vision is destructive. Passus I is, conversely, positive and constructive; it gives the dreamer the plain statement of faith which can help him out of, or, at least, *through* the clamorous evil of men and deeds. The teaching of Holy Church, the lady in white who comes slowly down from the 'Tower on a Toft' to instruct the wondering dreamer, says, in fact, all Langland is ever to say about life and God, and the way to salvation. She comes down from the hill where St. Truth, who is God, dwells, bearing God's own message, and foreshadows the theme and labour of the whole poem in her words on truth and love. The dreamer asks, significantly

> 'Teche me to no tresore.but telle me this ilke,
> How I may saue my soule.that seynt art yholden?'
>
> (B.I.83–4)

The reply comes in terms of truth and love, 'veritas' and 'via', truth and the way to approach truth—love:

> 'Whan alle tresores aren tried', quod she.'trewthe is the beste;'
>
> (*Ibid.*, 85)

and

> 'trewthe telleth that loue.is triacle of heuene.'[1]
>
> (*Ibid.*, 146)

The highest form of love, God's love for man which induced the sacrifice of Christ, is then defined by means of the imaginative metaphors of the linden-leaf and the needle; divine love required to take on flesh and blood, before it was fully satisfied.[2] And then nothing could withstand it:

> 'Was neuere leef vpon lynde.li3ter ther-after,
> And portatyf and persant.as the poynt of a nedle ...'
>
> (*Ibid.*, 154–5)

Love, therefore, is a link between man and God—God who

> 'Loked on vs with loue.and lete his sone deye
> Mekely for owre mysdedes.to amende vs alle;'
>
> (*Ibid.*, 165–6)

And she leaves the dreamer with these important words:

> 'Loue is leche of lyf.and nexte owre lorde selue,
> And also the graith gate.that goth in-to heuene;
> For-thi I sey as I seide.ere by the textis,
> Whan alle tresores ben ytryed.treuthe is the beste.'
>
> (B.I.202–5)

I think it is not an exaggeration to say that here, already, we have the elements out of which the poem is to be built. To attempt

[1] 'Truth says that love is heaven's elixir.' [2] See above, Chapter II, pp. 41–2.

to understand and remedy the evil state of things on the Field Full of Folk, the search for the 'treasure of truth', for St. Truth, or God, must be undertaken; the way to find truth goes through love— the 'triacle of heaven', the 'graith gate' to heaven. The negative, destructive side of Langland's vision is set against the positive, constructive; these two are to alternate throughout the poem— realism, satire, condemnation, analysis, set against idealism, faith, compassion, and synthesis. And the theme is defined as early as Passus I as the search for truth through love.

But as yet these things have only been set out didactically. The dreamer has received the teaching of Holy Church in all humility; he has not, however, experienced it—'felt in the blood and felt along the heart'. So the rest of the first section of the poem, Passus II–VII, is occupied with fuller investigation of the evil revealed in the Prologue. We are told this in the dreamer's words to Holy Church as she prepares to leave him:

'Kenne me bi somme crafte. to knowe the Fals . . .'
(B.II.4)

He must know more, probe deeper into the wound of sin. Therefore he becomes involved at closer range than before, with 'the false'. He sees the subtle working of the corrupt Lady Meed, who is both bribery and reward, among all classes of men; he sees and hears the confessions of the Seven Deadly Sins and their avowals of repentance. It is then time to move on to the positive view again; after Repentance, the way to amends. And now the theme of Truth, the 'treasure' described by Holy Church, is reintroduced. All the sinful decide to seek St. Truth—to set out to God.

A thousand of men tho. thrungen togyderes;
Criede vpward to Cryst. and to his clene moder
To haue grace to go with hem. Treuthe to seke.
(B.V.517–9)

But no one except the simple Plowman, Piers, knows the way, and he gives detailed directions. This is the second important positive stage in the poem's development. Piers, in Passus V, repeats the directions given to the dreamer in Passus I, both gathering up what has gone before, and affirming what is to come. He goes into fuller detail, however; the broad route to Truth through Love must be described more exactly for this crowd of confused pilgrims, who 'blustreden forth as bestes. over bankes and hilles' (B.V.521). The directions of Piers (B.V.568–647) have already been pointed out as worthy of close attention;[1] they are most significant, for in them Langland gives us vital clues to the development of the rest of the poem. Piers would send those who seek Truth, or God, through conscience, meekness and obedience, to the court of God—there mercy is the moat, the walls are buttressed with true belief, the bridge is prayer, the guardian of the door, grace. The pillars are penance, but the roofs are leaded with love. And if grace let you through, you may go in and find

> '. . . Treuthe sitte in thine herte,
> In a cheyne of charite. as thow a childe were . . .'

The way is not easy, but mercy will intercede for you—mercy which means Mary, and her son, Christ.

Here again, in a didactic fashion, we are told about the goal of Truth and the way to the goal. Through repentance, prayer and humility, by grace and mercy, we go to the Court of God, where the roof is made fast by love. And what we seek, whether we call it St. Truth, or God, we shall find mysteriously, at the end of the journey, in our own hearts. This is a concise statement of the main lines of exploration in the following three sections of the poem. The fact that the particular pilgrimage announced in Passus V does not *literally* take place, should not prevent us from seeing that the search for Truth, undertaken by the dreamer, Piers, and all kinds of allegorical creatures, is the predominant activity of the whole work: here we have a clear example of thematic as opposed to strictly narrative consistency. Dowel, Dobet and Dobest stand, like the Piers symbol, for many different things at various times in the poem, but they are basically and finally, only component parts of Truth itself: the quest for them is a quest for Truth on many spiritual levels.[2]

So Passus VIII–XV (Dowel) deal with the themes of repentance, obedience, humility, poverty; they show us the breaking down of sin in man, and, as a dramatic focus, the breaking down of sin in the dreamer himself, as he is pushed from one figure and from one encounter to another. The 'soure lof' of '*agite penitenciam*', set

---

[1] See above, pp. 31–2, and 86 foll.

[2] Professor Frank's statement in 'The Pardon Scene in *Piers Plowman*' *Speculum* XXVI (1951), p. 324, that 'whatever the search is for in Dowel, it is not for the way to Truth' seems to me indefensible. Professor Dunning, *op. cit.*, p. 232, rightly points out how, when the people on the 'field full of folk' are recalled by Hawkin (B. Passus XIII), 'we are reminded that the pilgrimage to Truth has been, in fact, for some time under way, but in a different mode. . . .'

before the dreamer at the Feast of Clergye (Passus XIII) must be devoured.

Passus XVI–XVIII (Dobet) through the magnificent re-enacted drama of the Passion and Death of Christ, the Resurrection and the Harrowing of Hell, convince us of the power of Grace and Mercy extended to man by Mary and Christ. By the end of Passus XVIII we are, indeed, 'roofed over by love'. At the same time, this section of the poem and the next, Passus XVIII–XX (Dobest) reveal to us dramatically, in the strange transformation of Piers, the once humble Plowman, the fact that 'truth sits in thy heart'. For Piers who comes to us at first, as the ordinary good man,[1] directing the pilgrims towards St. Truth, and offering to lead them to his shrine, shows himself, in the end, as the representative, even the repository of Divine Truth. His own words in Passus V foreshadow in a remarkable way what is actually to happen to him; he tells the pilgrims that if they would seek St. Truth, they must journey across the bridge of prayer and come face to face with the pillars of penance. So in Passus VII he sets out on his spiritual journey to Truth with prayers and penance:

'Of preyers and of penaunce. my plow shal ben herafter,
And wepen whan I shulde slepe . . .'

(B.VII.119–20)

From this moment onwards, his confident assertion that the pilgrim to Truth, if Grace has admitted him, will find Truth in his own heart, begins to be made good. As he, while absent, is defined afresh in terms of love and Christ, the divinity in him is growing and being revealed by the power of Grace. The striking and controversial line

. . . Piers the Plowman. *Petrus, id est, Christus.*

(B.XV.206)

shocks us into realization, and prepares us for the even more dramatic happenings of the rest of the poem, when one who is 'semblable . . . to Piers the Plowman . . .' (B.XVIII.10) jousts in Jerusalem, and dies for Man's sake, and when the search for Piers becomes as urgent a pilgrimage as the original search for St. Truth.

At Passus V this is still to come; we have only our directions. Now, once again, we and the dreamer must begin to *experience* directions, and no doubt, as this begins, unexpected checks and

---

[1] Although, as I have suggested above, he knows much more of spiritual mysteries than we expect of the ordinary good man (Dowel) at that stage.

complexities will be met with: in the characteristic manner of the
mediaeval preacher, Langland will explore many side-issues,
introduce many additional subjects. His themes must have fullest
expansion. But at this point, a broad indication of future development has been given. If we add to the teaching of Holy Church
in Passus I what Piers tells us in Passus V about the way to Truth,
we have all that is absolutely essential for our understanding
of Langland's intent. Dogmatically stated, the search is for St.
Truth or God, who was shown to us in the opening lines of the
poem, dwelling in the high 'tower on a toft'. The way to him
lies through repentance, cleansing from sin, but most powerfully
through love, which is Christ. Love is the basis of all lives, whether
they are defined as Dowel (good deeds), Dobet (prayer and self-
lessness) or Dobest (spiritual authority), and Christ's life is the
pattern for all lives—he lived by love.

The poem which announced as its first object the search for
Truth—a search to lead poet, dreamer and reader out of the maze
of the Field Full of Folk—comes more and more to focus upon the
nature of Christ, the means of attempting and succeeding in such
a search. By Passus V it is clear that Langland is reaching out to
Christ as the great solution of the problem; he, through the sacrifice
of love, bridged the gap between God and Man, between the Field
Full of Folk, and Truth in the Tower on a Toft. The search must
be undertaken in terms of Christ and love. Christ, this meeting
point of human and divine, welded all things into one. He, by
divine condescension became man and pilgrim; man, by the same
divine agency, is 'instinct with Godhead,' is, in fact, as much a part
of the goal as he is pilgrim. And the road along which God and
Man travel, is love.[1] The idea which is preoccupying Langland
even by Passus V can be expressed metaphorically, as the oneness,
the complete identification of pilgrim, pilgrimage, and goal through
the power of divine love. Naturally, the focus of such power lies
in the figure of Christ, who himself used the metaphor of the
journey and the journey's end:

I am the truth, the way, and the life.

[1] B.I.203. 'The graith gate·that goth in-to heuene', reinforced later, B.XI.179 foll.:
'For owre ioye and owre hele.Iesu Cryst of heuene,
In a pore mannes apparaille.pursueth vs euere . . .'

The expanded statement of that text in a poem of our own century can contribute something here:

> Thou art the Way:
> Hadst thou been nothing but the goal
> I know not, I,
> If thou hadst ever found my soul.
>
> I'll not reproach
> The road that winds, my feet that stir:
> Access, Approach art thou,
> Time, Way and Wayfarer.[1]

The plain proposition of the unity of 'goal, way and wayfarer' has been set out by Passus V; it remains for Langland to 'preve it in dede' as a poet and as a visionary. And this he does, mainly through the great imaginative concept of Piers—Christ, for it is as an entity, a composite symbol that Langland comes to regard and use both beings. His bold, and, at the same time, mysterious enlargements of the power and significance of Piers over the second part of the poem, until we begin to identify him with Christ,[2] his subsequent close association of Piers and Christ (Piers invokes Christ to fight the Devil,[3] Piers teaches Christ to heal and provide for himself on earth,[4] Piers is the armour in which Christ fights,[5] and Piers remains as Christ's authority on earth[6]) have, I think, no confusion in them. Piers and Christ become the two halves of a central truth, the two ways of seeing into a central mystery—man and God united in love, the pilgrim discovering Truth in his own heart. Over the first two sections of the poem we work, from the human vantage point, upwards; man, aspiring, catches a spark of the Divine, as Holy Church said firmly in Passus I: the Truth-led man

> is a god bi the gospel.agrounde and aloft. (*l.* 90)

And so we watch the metamorphosis of Piers as he becomes

> ... al one wiþ him in grace ...ȝit ... ful fer bineþe hym in kynde ...
> (*Cloud*, p. 120)

When, however, we near the third section, and the main revelation of the poem, the slant of vision changes. Now seeing God 'condescending into man' to complete that union, and seeing it not

[1] Alice Meynell, *Thou Art the Way*.
[2] In the '*Petrus, id est, Christus*' line, for instance (B.XV.206).
[3] B.XVI.87 foll.   [4] *Ibid.*, 103 foll.   [5] B.XVIII.22 foll.   [6] B.XIX.178 foll.

in the ineffable terms of the mystical treatises but in those of the life, death and triumph of Christ, Piers must be shown as the human material, the means through which the divine works:

> . . . a reasonable instrument wherin that He worketh.[1]

The living and speaking Piers must remain separate from the spiritual force which acts through him, just as the Crucifixion and the Harrowing of Hell must be effected by Christ, not Piers. The mystical writers, dealing habitually with such matters, express the distinction well:

> And I saw no difference between God and our Substance: but as it were all God: and yet mine understanding took that our Substance is in God: that is to say that God is God, and our Substance is a creature in God.[2]

Langland has a far more difficult problem of expression to solve; starting with his conviction that, by grace, God is within, he has to show us in dramatic allegory how the 'creature in God' and God interact on all levels of truth.

And now, after tracing some of the paths of that allegory, we may inquire whether an over-all multiple meaning for the poem can still be defended. I think it can. As far as the second mode of significance, the allegorical, is concerned, the poem examines powerfully the special relationship of man and Christ: Christ the Redeemer, the way to God, the moat of Mercy, the pilgrim Piers, who is both human and divine. On the one hand, it tells us of the mercy and love of Christ; on the other, of the power given to man by this love and mercy. This is Piers the pilgrim, the guide, and the way. As far as the third level is concerned, the tropological, moral sense, the poem teaches on the Christian virtues around which a man's life should be set—selflessness, patience, charity. It shows how sin can be cleansed through prayer and repentance: so the Seven Deadly Sins repent, the cloak of the ordinary unreformed man, Hawkin, is scoured fresh, and he is set on the right path.[3]

---

[1] Hilton, *Scale of Perfection*, Bk. II, Chapter 24: see above, p. 89.

[2] Dame Julian of Norwich, *op. cit.*, Chapter LIV. Once we regard Piers and Christ as a *dual* operation or activity, many of the difficulties found by critics in their relationship are removed. In this light, Professor Frank's statement that 'the context does not allow us to go beyond this view of a human Piers' (*Piers Plowman*, p. 117) has only a half-truth in it. Langland's own doubts about the propriety of some of his references to Piers in the B Text (*Petrus, id est, Christus*, for instance) which may prompt omissions in the C revision, can be variously explained. His emendations in C are as often the result of extreme cautiousness as they are of basic disagreement, and the B text stands consistent—though daring, perhaps, in approach. See Donaldson, *op. cit.*, Chapter VI.

[3] B.XIII.272 foll.

Piers willingly subjects himself to rigorous spiritual discipline[1] and the dreamer, in the second section of the poem, is in constant process of correction.[2] Moreover, there is abundant positive instruction, 'good at every level'; by the end of the poem we know what a Christian life should be, whether it is Dowel, Dobet or Dobest.

When we turn to the fourth level, the anagogical, mystical significance, the poem 'shadows forth' how the mystic's life develops—from active good deeds, to dissatisfaction with this (as Piers turns from ploughing to prayer in Passus VII) on to harsher disciplines (the self-analysis, the difficult inquiries of Passus VIII–XV). Then comes the gradual revelation of God's love; the discovery, by means of love, of God or Truth within the soul. What the dreamer learns and Piers experiences is here described by a writer dealing with the greatest of all the spiritual teachers of the Middle Ages:

. . . to love Him as He loves Himself, to love Him as He loves us, and by the gift of that very love with which He loves Himself and loves us—that, truly, . . . is to have God in us.[3]

Kynde's command to the dreamer, towards the end of the poem,

'Lerne to loue . . . and leue of alle othre . . .'
(B.XX.207)

is, in this deepest sense, a direction of ultimate importance for

. . . the very affection of love is the sole possible substitute here below for the vision of God which we lack, and love therefore in us stands for vision.[4]

A direct vision of God the poem certainly does not give us; it does give, however, in the Piers-Christ relationship, and in the endless drama of the Passion, Resurrection and Harrowing of Hell, an account of the nature and operation of the love which 'stands for vision', and an intimation of the divine source of that love. It has, moreover, a proper end for such a high process. The return to the Field Full of Folk is in keeping with the main stream of Western spirituality; the practical fruits of illumination are gathered not only in the individual soul, but in outward-going service of others. The building of the Barn of Unity (B. Passus XIX) is no deviation from course; one of its symbolic meanings is the foundation of

---

[1] B.VII.117 foll.
[2] As at the Feast of Learned Doctors, for instance, B.XIII.22 foll.
[3] Gilson, *The Mystical Theology of St. Bernard*, p. 149.
[4] *Loc. cit.*

faith upon vision, the resumption of earthly toil with a new sense of purposefulness. Then, if the general progress of the poem can be said to correspond to the stages of the mystical way, the whole matter is centred for us in the figure of Piers, whose changing significance can only be comprehended naturally in terms of a mystical alchemy:

... þe eendles merueilous miracle of loue, þe whiche schal neuer take eende.

But for all of these meanings the poem has a fitting conclusion. At a first reading, we may feel that everything has been lost; we started on the Field Full of Folk, we return to it. Langland ends by showing us Holy Church once more beset by evil; Piers has vanished, and we are to search all over again. Many writers have felt that the weight of failure rested heavily upon Langland at this point.[1] Admittedly, on one level of meaning, there is realism, even pessimism in the ending Langland gives us. He was convinced, no doubt, that in the England of his day spiritual authority had vanished: contrition was sleeping:

> 'He lith and dremeth,' seyde Pees.'and so do many other;
> The frere with his phisik.this folke hath enchaunted,
> And plastred hem so esyly[2].thei drede no synne.
> (B.XX.375–7)

But the idea of the search beginning once more has, in more important ways, a great optimism in it. It may symbolize the renewed effort to establish proper contact between man and Christ, the renewed effort to live the good moral life, to embark upon the intimate journey to God in the stillness of contemplation and to bring others the fruits of that journey. It is most probably all these things, but whatever particular interpretation we give it, the search begins again with resolve. Like the dreamer, like 'our first parents' in *Paradise Lost*, we have full knowledge at last of our terms of reference; we know the place we stand in, the path to take, and our destination—we are still pilgrims, but we 'know our country',

> We shall not cease from exploration,
> And the end of all our exploring
> Will be to arrive where we started
> And know the place for the first time.

[1] Professor Kane, *op. cit.*, p. 244, thinks that the ideal formulated by the poet was so high 'that he as much as acknowledges the impossibility of attaining it, and thus brings his search to an end'.
[2] '... and has poulticed them so comfortably ...'

Moreover, we are sure that we are capable of journeying, however feeble our powers, for Piers-Christ is the Way as well as the Goal. Whether we shall arrive at the deepest, mystic apprehension of St. Truth or not, we can all travel

> . . . wiþ þe draw3t of þis loue and þe voise of þis cleping.
> (*The Cloud*, p. 14)

'with the drawing of this love, and the voice of this calling', with Piers the Plowman, 'who has set all sciences at a sop, save love alone'.

APPENDIX

THE VERSIONS OF *PIERS PLOWMAN*

PIERS PLOWMAN has come down to us in three recensions: the A text (written about 1370) contains a Prologue and twelve Passus, the B text (written between 1377 and 1379) is expanded to a Prologue and twenty Passus, and the C text (written between 1380 and 1399) is expanded still further to a Prologue and twenty-three Passus.[1]

The B and C versions represent fairly thorough reworkings of the poem: B expanded A's 2400 lines to 3200, and added over 4000 lines, thus reaching a total length of over 7200. C revised practically the whole of B, leaving only the last two Passus untouched, and lengthening the poem by about 100 lines.

Critical debate has been much occupied with the problems of authorship raised by the existence of these three versions, and it is fortunate for *Piers Plowman* studies that Professor Kane's monograph on the subject has so authoritatively supported single authorship.[2]

poem (*Piers Plowman; The C Text and its Poet*), Ch. VII.[2]

There are strong reasons for beginning a comprehensive reading of *Piers Plowman* with the B text. A is mainly of interest as a preliminary 'essay' in a major project: C represents a further development and, in some ways, a refinement, of tendencies already noticeable in B, but an appreciation of both its virtues and its deficiencies can only be gained through familiarity with B. It is possible, moreover, that it is not a completed revision; the lack of alteration in the last two Passus may mean that the poet was interrupted in his task—perhaps by death. The B version gives us a completed text which is satisfactory as an introduction to Langland's characteristic thought and methods of work. It has one considerable advantage over the C version for the new reader of the poem: it contains a higher proportion of imaginative verse writing. With some exceptions, the tendency of the C reviser was to reduce or substitute for such passages. On the other hand, the differences

---

[1] See J. A. W. Bennett, 'The Date of the A-Text of *Piers Plowman*', *P.M.L.A.*, LVIII (1943) and 'The Date of the B-Text of *Piers Plowman*', *M.Aev.* XII (1943). For the C-Text, see E. T. Donaldson, *op. cit.*, pp. 18–19, 'A Note on the Date of the C-Text.'

[2] Kane, *Piers Plowman. The Evidence for Authorship, op. cit.*, p. 72.

between B and C are not so dramatic as to make the B text unrepresentative of Langland's mature intentions.

It has been pointed out in the course of this study that Langland is first and last a poet whose art is controlled by the need to communicate religious ideas and experiences; his willingness to dispense with 'pure poetry' is already marked in the B text. In fact, none of the various revisions which distinguish text C can surprise us greatly if we are quite familiar with the nature of text B. The very difficulty of generalizing about the motives behind the revisions links B and C: if the unqualified statement of 'moralist predominant over poet' is inadequate for B, it is inadequate, to some extent, for C also. If the poet of C seems anxious to delete or transform the 'poetry' of B, he also chooses to add, on occasion, verse of high imaginative power.

Some of the main principles of the B to C revision are set out below: the reader is referred, however, to the detailed discussion and illustration of these principles in E. Talbot Donaldson's study of the C text.

(a) Clarification or further illustration of points in B.
e.g. C.IV.317 foll.: the poet adds about 92 lines on the subject of 'meed', making sure that his audience understands the nature of various kinds of reward or payment, and, in particular, the nature of 'mede and mercede'.

(b) Reduction of ambiguous or dramatically phrased elements in B.
e.g. the coupling of Piers with Christ, '*Petrus, id est, Christus*' in B.XV.206 does not occur in the equivalent portion of C.XVII.

(c) Reduction of passages in B which refer directly to the contemporary social scene.
e.g. B.X.94 foll.: the C text omits from Passus XII the censure of lords and ladies for 'new-fangled' habits of living.

(d) Reduction of passages of personal import in B.
e.g. B.XII.16 foll.: The justification of Langland's work as a poet is omitted from C.XV.

(e) Substitution for lines of immediate poetic appeal in B which may yet be capable of misapprehension or may encourage the placing of false emphases.

e.g. B.Prol. 1–10: the pleasing but strictly conventional dream-introduction is considerably shortened and revised in C.

e.g. B.II.11–17: the rich description of Lady Meed is simplified in C.

It is worth recording, however, that although the poet of C adheres to these principles fairly consistently, there are important exceptions. He adds a very moving passage of social commentary on the plight of the poor in contemporary England (C.X.71 foll.) and a detailed and lengthy autobiographical statement (C.VI.1 foll.). Some of his shorter emendations are in the direction of greater vividness and imaginative range: compare C.IX.45–6.

> At churche in the charnel.cheorles aren vuel to knowe,
> Other a knyght fro a knaue.other a queyne fro a queene.

with B.VI.50–51

> For in charnel atte chirche.cherles ben vuel to knowe,
> Or a kniȝte fram a knaue there.knowe this in thin herte.

As a more extensive example, C.XXI.362 foll., from the Harrowing of Hell episode, improves upon the equivalent B version for stylistic grace and power.

SELECT BIBLIOGRAPHY

a) EDITIONS

The Vision of William concerning Piers the Plowman, in Three Parallel Texts, ed. W. W. Skeat (Oxford, 1886), 2 vols., reprinted 1954 with a bibliographical note by Dr. J. A. W. Bennett.

A text:
>   (i) *Piers the Plowman; a critical edition of the A version* by T. A. Knott and D. C. Fowler (Baltimore, 1952).
>   (ii) *Will's Visions of Piers Plowman and Do-wel,* ed. G. Kane (London, 1960).

B text:
>   *The Vision of William concerning Piers the Plowman. Text B.* ed. W. W. Skeat (Oxford, 1869, reprinted 1950).

C text:
>   *An Attempt to Approach the C-Text of Piers Plowman* by F. A. R. Carnegy (London, 1934). Contains a text of Passus II, III, and IV.
>   E. Salter and D. Pearsall, *Piers Plowman* (York Medieval Texts, 1967). Long extracts ranging over the whole poem are presented.

b) MODERNIZATIONS

H. W. Wells, *The Vision of Piers Plowman* (London, 1935, reprinted 1945).
N. Coghill, *Visions from Piers Plowman* (London, 1949).
D. and R. Attwater, *The Book Concerning Piers the Plowman* (Everyman, 1957).
(All of the above translations are in verse.)
J. F. Goodridge, *Piers the Ploughman* (Penguin, 1959, reprinted 1960).
(A prose version.)

c) CRITICAL STUDIES AND ARTICLES

M. W. Bloomfield, *Piers Plowman as a Fourteenth Century Apocalypse* (New Brunswick, N.J., 1963).
J. A. Burrow, 'The Audience of *Piers Plowman*', *Anglia*, LXXV (1957).
R. W. Chambers, *Man's Unconquerable Mind* (London, 1939), pp. 88–171.
N. Coghill, 'The Character of Piers Plowman Considered from the B-Text', *M.Aev.*, II (1933).
—— 'The Pardon of Piers Plowman', *British Academy Gollancz Lecture* (1945), *Proc. Brit. Acad.*, XXX (1944).
C. Dawson, *Mediaeval Religion* (London, 1935), Part III, 'The Vision of Piers Plowman'.
E. T. Donaldson, *Piers Plowman; The C-Text and its Poet* (New Haven, 1949).
T. P. Dunning, *Piers Plowman: An Interpretation of the A-text* (Dublin, 1937), 'The Structure of the B-Text of *Piers Plowman*', *R.E.S.*, N.S. VII (1956).
R. W. Frank, *Piers Plowman and the Scheme of Salvation* (New Haven, 1957).
G. Hort, *Piers Plowman and Contemporary Religious Thought* (London, 1938).

S. S. Hussey, 'Langland, Hilton and the Three Lives', *R.E.S.*, N.S. VII (1956):
G. Kane, *Middle English Literature: a Critical Study of the Romances, the Religious Lyrics and Piers Plowman* (London, 1951).
J. Lawlor, 'The Imaginative Unity of *Piers Plowman*', *R.E.S.*, N.S. VIII (1957).
—— *Piers Plowman. An Essay in Criticism* (London, 1962).
D. L. Owen, *Piers Plowman. A Comparison with some earlier and contemporary French Allegories* (London, 1912).
D. W. Robertson and B. F. Huppé, *Piers Plowman and Scriptural Tradition* (Princeton, 1951).
E. Salter, 'Medieval Poetry and the Figural View of Reality', *British Academy Gollancz Lecture* for 1968.
A. H. Smith, *Piers Plowman and the Pursuit of Poetry* (London, 1950).
A. C. Spearing, *Criticism and Medieval Poetry* (London, 1964).
D. A. Traversi, 'The Vision of Piers Plowman', *Scrutiny*, V (1936–7).
H. W. Wells, 'The Construction of *Piers Plowman*', *P.M.L.A.*, XLIV (1929).
—— 'The Philosophy of *Piers Plowman*', *P.M.L.A.*, LIII (1938).
E. Zeeman (Salter), 'Piers Plowman and the Pilgrimage to Truth', *Essays and Studies* (1958).

(d) RELATED STUDIES IN THE HISTORY, RELIGION AND LITERATURE OF THE PERIOD
E. Auerbach, *Mimesis*, tr. W. R. Trask (N. York, 1957).
D. Bethurum, (ed.) *Critical Approaches to Mediæval Literature* (Columbia University Press, 1960).
E. de Bruyne, *Études d'Esthétique Médiévale* (Brugge, 1946), 3 parts.
D. Everett, *Essays on Middle English Literature* (Oxford, 1955).
E. Gilson, *The Mystical Theology of St. Bernard*, tr. A. H. C. Downes (London, 1940).
—— *Les Idées et Les Lettres* (Paris, 1932).
D. Knowles, *The English Mystical Tradition* (London, 1961).
M. McKisack, *The Fourteenth Century*, 1307–99 (Oxford, 1959).
J. P. Oakden, *Alliterative Poetry in Middle English.* (Part I) *The Dialectal and Metrical Survey* (Manchester, 1930).
—— (Part II) *A Survey of the Traditions* (Manchester, 1935, reprinted 1937).
G. R. Owst, *Preaching in Mediaeval England* (Cambridge, 1926)
—— *Literature and Pulpit in Mediaeval England* (Cambridge, 1933).
W. A. Pantin, *The English Church in the Fourteenth Century* (Cambridge, 1955).
E. Salter, 'The Alliterative Revival', *M.P.*, LXIV, nos. 2 and 3 (1966, 1967).
B. Smalley, *The Study of the Bible in the Middle Ages* (Oxford, 1952), 2nd ed.
R. H. Tawney, *Religion and the Rise of Capitalism* (London, 1926).
G. M. Trevelyan, *England in the Age of Wycliffe* (London, 1929), 4th ed.

INDEX

Abbey of the Holy Ghost, pp. 69, 76-7, 80-1.
Allegory:
  multiple interpretation, pp. 5-6, 65-70, 81, 102-5.
  flexible usages, pp. 6, 70-81.
Alliterative verse tradition:
  audience, p. 23.
  defining characteristics, pp. 15-21.
  geographical factors, pp. 22-3.
Ancrene Riwle, pp. 79-80.

Bosch, Hieronymus, pp. 71-2.

Capgrave, John, p. 25.
Chaucer:
  use of alliterative style, p. 13.
  use of dreams, p. 59.
  Canterbury Tales, p. 28.
  Book of the Duchess, pp. 59, 91.
  House of Fame, p. 59.
  Troilus and Criseyde, p. 28.
Cleanness, pp. 18, n.1, 19.
Cloud of Unknowing, pp. 63, 64, 81, and n.2, 84, 85, 101, 104, 105.
Cursor Mundi, p. 46.

Dante, pp. 69, 77, n.1.
Desert of Religion, pp. 69, 76-7, 80-1.
Dreams:
  the secular dream-convention, pp. 58-9.
  the religious vision, pp. 9, 59-62.
  the poet-dreamer, pp. 91-2.

Eliot, T. S., pp. 3, 44-5, 64, 95, 104.

Figura verborum, pp. 29, 37-40.

Gascoigne, Dr. Thomas, pp. 25-6.

Hilton, Walter, *The Scale of Perfection*, pp. 61, 80, 82, 85-9, 102.
Hugh of St. Victor, p. 67.

John of Wales, p. 29.
Julian of Norwich, *The Revelations of Divine Love*, pp. 34, 36, 88, n.1, 89, and n.2, 102.

Laȝamon, *The Brut*, p. 23.
Love, Nicholas, *The Mirror of the Blessed Life of Jesu Christ*, pp. 25, n.1, 26, 67, n.4, 82-3.

Macrobius, *Commentary* on the *Somnium Scipionis*, p. 58.
Meynell, Alice, p. 101.
Metaphor, pp. 41-3.
Milton, pp. 1-2, 45.
Miracle Plays, pp. 2, 46, 89.
Mirror of St. Edmund, p. 82.
Morte Arthure, pp. 16, 19, 21, 38.
Mum and the Sothsegger, p. 23.
Mystical prose, pp. 81-90.

Patience, pp. 16, 18, n.1.
Pearl, pp. 18, n.1, 59, 60, n.2, 77-8.

Rhetoric:
  alliterative rhetoric, pp. 16-18.
  Chaucerian rhetoric, p. 17.
  pulpit rhetoric, pp. 26-7, 29.
  artes poeticae, pp. 17, and n.2, 18, 27, 29, 30.
  artes praedicandi, pp. 26-30.
Robert of Basevorn, p. 29.
Robert of Melun, p. 29.
Rolle, Richard, p. 82.
Roman de la Rose, pp. 58, 77.
Ruysbroeck, John, p. 90, n.1.

St. Bernard, pp. 61, 62, 85, 89, n.1, 92-3.
St. Erkenwald, p. 15, n.1.
Sermons:
  methods of procedure, pp. 6, 26-30, 48.
  occurrence in *Piers Plowma*, pp. 48-57.
Sir Gawain and the Green Knight, pp. 15, n.3, 18, and n.4, 23, 38.

Translated devotional prose: theory and practice, pp. 24-6.

William of Palerne, p. 23, and n.3.
Winner and Waster, pp. 14, n.2, 17, 23.